Barnsley's History
FROM THE AIR
1926-1939

Barnsley's History FROM THE AIR 1926-1939

Brian Elliott

Wharncliffe Publishing Limited

First published in 1994 by
Wharncliffe Publishing Limited

Copyright © Wharncliffe Publishing Limited 1994

For up-to-date information on other titles produced
under the Wharncliffe imprint, please telephone or
write to:

Wharncliffe Publishing Limited
FREEPOST
47 Church Street, Barnsley
South Yorkshire S70 2BR
Telephone (24 hours): 01226-734555

ISBN: 1-871647-185

A CIP catalogue record of this book is available from the British Library.

Cover photograph: Change of role for this D.H.9A ex-bomber seen here
employed as an aerial photographer's platform during the 1920s. Peace time
purposes were found for aerial photography which had been perfected over
the battlefields of Europe during the recent conflict.

Printed in Great Britain by Redwood Books, Trowbridge, Wiltshire

CONTENTS

INTRODUCTION

Aerial photography has never been so popular, especially in familiar settings. Wes Hobson's current series of colour aerial photographs has received considerable public interest from readers of the *Barnsley Chronicle*. On the ground our perception is obscured by the distraction of urban and natural features. Even from the vantage point of the top deck of a bus we are able to see beyond the boundaries of normal vision. The recorded view from a light aircraft reveals the overall pattern of streets and houses, providing us with an instant appreciation of the form and layout of our built environment — though individual buildings demand more diligent study. As when examining a large-scale map, care is needed in order to re-adjust our familiarity with three-dimensional features but the results can be very rewarding. Ideally, a combination of map, aerial photograph and on the ground observation leads to a better understanding of the landscape. For further detail we must also recognise the wealth of oral history around us which can make visits to libraries and archives much more meaningful for the researcher.

Although many features come to life on aerial photographs questions are often raised. Certain buildings, streets or even neighbourhoods may have been transformed by subsequent re-development. This is why collections of urban aerial photographs are of such value to the historian and family historian as well as having an obvious appeal to anyone wanting a reminder of an environment that may have changed almost beyond recognition. Yet the perspective is so wide that even the most up-to-date aerial view can yield vital clues about past townscapes and certainly historical landscapes — as archaeologists have so often found.

Historical aerial photographs of Barnsley are very important since they offer us a unique opportunity to glimpse the town before the major changes of the post-war years. The original idea of the publisher was for relatively brief captions to be added to more than fifty aerial views from the 1920s to the present-day. Beginning the research, however, soon demonstrated that a more detailed commentary over a shorter period and, where possible, the use of contemporary groundshots would hopefully result in a more meaningful presentation. In the event the information and comments of Barnsley and ex-Barnsley people may be of at least equal interest.

This book would not have been possible but for access to one of the most remarkable collections of aerial photographs in the United Kingdom. The Aerofilms Library contains more than half a million photographs dating from around 1920 to the present day. The equipment and aircraft were crude by modern standards. Plate cameras were used for the 1920s photographs, producing 5 x 4 glass negatives which had to be individually loaded into the camera for each exposure. Bearing in mind that the early aircraft were open-seater biplanes it is a remarkable testimony to the crew that such high quality results were obtained.

Some of the aerial views shown in the book were probably a consequence of contract work but others were certainly 'random' sorties adding to the immense portfolio of Aerofilms. This collection relates mainly to the early years of aerial photography when sceptics in both authority and in public may have had suspicions over motives. In 1924, for example, Aerofilm founder F.L. Wills was interviewed by Scotland Yard who confiscated some of his aerial photographs and threatened him with imprisonment since he was in danger of contravening the Official Secrets Act! In the 1930s Aerofilms were accused by one individual for photographing the roof-tops of country houses to aid cat-burglars. It is pleasing that such suspicions were overcome as we now have a most important aerial record of the changing face of our town and district.

Brian Elliott

Left: An Aerofilms photographer poses for the camera during the early 1930s, before climbing into the open cockpit of his Klemm L25 monoplane. Note the camera aperture under the fuselage, between the undercarriage wheels, with the small metal wind shield. *(Aerofilms)* **B1264**

ACKNOWLEDGEMENTS

I am grateful to Aerofilms Limited for permission to reproduce copies of their aerial photographs and special thanks are due to Aerofilm librarian Michael Willis who has been most helpful. The production of the book has been in the hands of Wharncliffe's Book Design Manager Roni Wilkinson and his cheerful assistant Caroline Cox, both of whom have put up with my frequent requests with typical Barnsley humour — and a great deal of hard work. Thanks are also due to Timothy Hewitt, Managing Director, for initiating the project and keeping faith with it even though publication has taken longer than anticipated.

Many people and several organisations have responded to my requests for information over the last two years. I would particularly like to thank the following: Peter Ashman, Dr Denis Ashurst, Jim Badics, Constance Banks, Ernest Barker, Beatson Clark of Stairfoot, Don Booker, Arthur Boylan, Freda Brooke, Mr T.H. Brown, Dorothy Charlesworth, the Cutts family, Mr R. Grayson, Alan Hall, Ian Harley, Leslie Hennel, Maurice Hepworth (Barnsley Local Studies Librarian), Molly Hill, John Hislop (Barnsley M.B.C.), Norman Moody, Freda Newman, Maureen Ogden, Mr H. Oxley, Steve Prest, Lorraine Raybold (Yorkshire Traction Company), Walter Ridley, Tanya Schmoller, Harold Taylor, W.A. Taylor, Mr W.H. Stewart, John Threlkeld, Anne Turton, Ruth Vyse and Gillian Nixon (Barnsley Archives), Cyril Walton, Eric Watling, Mrs W. Wigglesworth, Neil York and family. Some photographs (with acknowledgement) have been used from the Tasker Collection and I am ever grateful to Mrs Mary Tasker for permission to reproduce them in this form. Picture credits are shown relevant to each illustration used but any uncredited remain the copyright of Wharncliffe Publishing and Barnsley Chronicle.

REFERENCES TO AERIAL PHOTOGRAPHS

Plate		Plate	
1	21098	8	57294
2	21103	9	55897
3	18225	10	61493
4	21104	11	61495
5	16299	12	A153071
6	18208	13	A106556 & R15270
7	57290	14	48005

Front Cover: **C325**
Rear Cover: **57290**

Many heads turned skywards on a sunny Tuesday in May 1928, drawn by the relatively unfamiliar sight and sound of a low-flying aircraft. The legacy of this photographic sortie is one of the earliest aerial images of central Barnsley, conserved and carefully printed by Aerofilms from a sixty-five year old glass negative. The photograph gives us unparalleled views of streets and buildings; and captures that part of town which was to experience so much change in the ensuing years. In 1928 Barnsley, like other industrial towns, had begun to respond to inevitable changes after the Great War; but the pace was not so advanced as to hide its historic function as a bustling market and retail centre.

The focus of activity on Wednesdays and Saturdays was of course the famous market, jammed full of character and with a reputation for bargains so renown that visitors flocked from far and wide. Neat rows of market stalls can be seen on May Day Green, forming a large and small triangle, separated by Kendray Street. Coming to Barnsley by tram, omnibus or on foot had become a shopping ritual that some people will still remember. The Kendray estate, which occupied land between Eldon Street and Cheapside, had been

Below: The Fish Market. *(Tasker Collection)*

Right: 1:25,000 O.S. Map. *(1903)*

Above: The Cross Keys Hotel. *(Tasker Collection)*
Below: The 'Fruit Market' on a busy day

purchased in 1874, enabling a much needed enlargement of the trading area. The west side of Kendray Street first served as the new cattle mart, but by the 1920s had become the popular fish market, reached either from Kendray Street or (down the steps) from Eldon Street. The cattle market moved to a more spacious location to the north of Queens Road, (formerly Jumble Lane) where the business of farmers was intermingled with the cries of hawkers and occasional sellers of quack remedies. This area, formerly occupied by Robinson's Saw Mill was also known as the 'bottom market' and became noted for the wholesale trade of fruit and vegetables.

Barnsley had long outgrown its small medieval market place, though the old hill continued to be used by traders in an attractive setting overlooked by family businesses with still familiar names: Guest, Moorhouse, Elstone and Hirst; but emerging multiple retailers such as W.H. Smith (established here in 1906) and Boots Ltd. (1923) were also evident. The site of the Corn Exchange, destroyed by a fire in December, 1927, can just be seen at the corner of Market Hill and Shambles Street . Opened by a private company in 1852, it offered spacious and dry accommodation for farmers and dealers to display cereal samples, enabling the town to compete with neighbouring urban centres. Bought by the council in 1872, the handsome building was a sad loss to the town as it had become a valuable public asset, used for meetings, concerts and civic occasions.

We are given fine views of two principal shopping streets: Cheapside and Eldon Street. The oldest, Cheapside, was occupied in the late eighteenth century by small workshops housing craftsmen such as wiremakers, nailmakers, shoemakers, feltmakers, breechesmakers and joiners, where 'making' combined with selling, the only exception being Thomas Beckett's substantial grocer's shop. From the 1860s retailers were attracted to Cheapside to be near the expanding

Above: Cheapside in the Golden Age of the tram *(Elliott Collection)*

new market. The era after the First World War was one of contradictions. For some it was a time to dance the Charleston, for many others to escape to the picture palace, away from the disillusionment and poverty of the General Strike when miners were left to fight alone before being forced to return to work because of extreme hardship. It was certainly a time of great commercial change. Of twenty-two Cheapside shops in 1928, only ten could trace their occupancy before 1914; the oldest being Edward Bailey's 'We Supply all but the Baby' drapery, opened in 1883, and still in business in nearby New Street. New proprietors included butchers' Albert Hirst (1923) and Arthur Cooke (1921); whilst Crowes' Tailors (1928) had to compete with the likes of Montague Burton Ltd. (1928), Alexandre Ltd (1925)

and Barnsley British Co-operative Society's brand new outfitting department.

Eldon Street, created in 1840, is mainly in full sun, with traders' blinds in place. The Yorkshire Penny Bank building can be seen at the junction with Market Hill and there is a good view of the upper facade of Benjamin Harral's famous 'Ring Shop' , established here in 1906 where generations of local folk purchased their love-tokens. The Y.M.C.A. building , opened in 1909, had three shops beneath it, in 1928 occupied by Holroyds' (cleaners), Walkers' (outfitters) and Halfords' new cycle shop. Nearby, small businesses such as G. Bell's tobacconists and (next to Warner Gothard's photographic studio) T.W. Brown's ironmongers, continued to serve Barnsley shoppers until about 1960.

Above: Cheapside and Queen Street in about 1915

Above: Benjamin Harral's famous 'Ring Shop'. *(Tasker Collection)*

Below: Market stalls on the south side of Queens Road. *(Tasker Collection)*

The entry into Barnsley Arcade, made in 1893, was flanked by one of the newer tobacconist shops, S. Tetley & Son (1926-57) and local historian and naturalist Edwin Bayford's single storey drapery emporium which extended to the Public Hall. The latters ground floor housed several shops including hairdresser J. R. Holmes (later Beachills), Billington's chemists, fruiterer E. Hattersley, the Singer Sewing Machine shop, drapers Ford & Hutchinson and the well-known Haigh Brothers newsagency.

The Public (and Mechanics) Hall was built by a private company in 1876-7 at a cost of £27,000 but twelve years later was gifted to the town by Charles Harvey, J.P. It was by far the largest and most imposing of Barnsley's buildings. By the twenties it had a multipurpose role,

Above: The Harvey Institute (Public Hall), Eldon Street, celebrates a royal occasion. *(Elliott Collection)*

Below: Laying the tram-lines, Kendray Street, c.1901 *Dennis Gill*

accommodating the School of Art, Free Library and growing Technical School; and was a popular venue for concerts, lectures, meetings, balls and of course 'animated picture shows'. Jack Hylton and his Band performed at the hall on May 17th, 1928, seats costing one to three shillings (5-15p), including tea. Barnsley's first 'talkie' picture, *Mother's Baby*, starring Morton Downey, was shown here in 1929.

The facade of the Empire 'Super Cinema', with its great self-advertising hoarding, is also in view, just a few yards from the Public Hall. The main film was a western, *Trembling River* described in the *Barnsley Chronicle* as 'A characteristic drama of the great ranches', featuring Tom Mix and "Tony" the wonder horse. Opened in 1909, hundreds queued to see the great silent stars of the early post-war era: Chaplin, Valentino, Keaton, the zany Keystone Kops, Harold Lloyd and Mary Pickford, not to the accompaniment of a lone piano, but 'The Empire Orchestra', under the direction of Mr F. Jervis. The building succumbed to fire in 1954 but was replaced by the Gaumont, now Odeon Cinema.

Returning to the Market Hill end of Eldon Street, we can see the backs of old properties at the junction with Queens Street. E. Nash's Chemist shop occupied the corner, with the jeweller G.W. Argus and tailor F. Harrison in Queens Street, all replaced in 1930 by Montague Burton's gleaming 'white' edifice.

South-facing properties, on May Day Green, also with their blinds down included Jacksons Ltd (Hatters), Benjamin Gaunt and Son (Jewellers), Piper's Penny Bazaar and Hunter's Tea Store. We also have a fine view of the Cross Keys Hotel which was demolished in 1972. Mr James Cressey was licensee of this mid-Victorian establishment from 1924 to 1960. The Public Weigh House, looked after by caretaker Charles Roe, can be seen next to the hotel, surmounted by a bell which was rung to mark the closing of the market. The rooftop of the nearby Wellington Hotel is also apparent .

By Edwardian times Regent Street had become the principal business area of the developing town. Fine Victorian private residences were converted into offices by legal and medical practices, accountants, estate agents and insurance companies. New offices were also built to accommodate the growing need for professional services. At the top of the street, for example, old warehouses were cleared to make way for the south-facing office block which can be seen at the junction with Eastgate. Across the road stood the Central Post Office, built in 1882. Next door was the more subdued facade of the offices of Raley and Pratt and, at the corner with Royal Street, the old premises of Barnsley Permanent Building Society. There is also a fine view of the National Provincial (now Royal Bank of Scotland) Bank at the junction of Royal Street and Church Street.

At the junction with Eastgate we have a clear view of the dignified County Court, erected in 1871. The tower and lofty spire of the Gothic Congregational chapel of 1856 is a most striking feature whilst part of the Court House Station (opened in 1870 but built as a court in 1861) is just in shot, completing a trio of grand public buildings occupying the south side of the street.

A well-defined industrial zone can be seen to the south of Queens Road and west of May Day Green. Prior to its development this area was mainly open space but came alive for the February and May Fairs. This was a traditional venue for the sale of horses and cattle whilst a market for pigs was held on Moorside, near the bottom of Swinhill Field Road (Queens Road). The town gasworks, founded in 1821, is a distinctive feature, lending its name to a noted Barnsley street lost in the 1960s redevelopment of the area: the Gas Nook. The Borough Electricity Works, with cooling towers visible, was established in Beckett Square in 1900. It sold power to the Barnsley and District Traction Company which, in 1902, began operating a shuttle service of trams from Smithies (near the Old Mill Gasworks) via Barnsley to

Below: When the aerial photograph was taken 8 May, 1928, Tuesday, popular cowboy hero Tom Mix was drawing the crowds at the Empire.

THE EMPIRE
SUPER CINEMA, BARNSLEY.

MON., TUES. & WED., MAY 7, 8 & 9.

May Robson, Phyllis Haver, Harrison Ford and Franklyn Langhorn in THE

REJUVENATION OF AUNT MARY
A Sparkling Motor Race Comedy.

TOM MIX
with "TONY," in TUMBLING RIVER.
A Characteristic Drama of the Great Ranches.

THE EMPIRE ORCHESTRA, under the direction
JERVIS.

11 & 12.

Worsbrough Bridge and Dale at one or two (old) pence per journey. Joseph Barraclough's name is just descernable on the rooftop of the former Union Foundry, converted into warehouses and shops after the First

World War. We are also afforded a good view of the white painted front and gable end of the Corporation Hotel on Pontefract Road, built in 1844 as the Dusty Miller. John Henry Brown had the licence in 1928; and there is a good view of the side of the Wire Trellis Hotel prior to a face lift. Fred Moxon had just become landlord.

The elevated railway, established by the Midland company in 1870, entered a station built at the back of the Court House. A steam train on the older (1851) line can be seen approaching the Jumble Lane crossing, about to pass under the foot bridge, before entering Exchange Station (out of shot). The railways were of course essential to the economic development of Barnsley during the Victorian period and by the twenties were patronized by thousands of holidaymakers. A day trip to Blackpool, for example, cost five shillings return (25p) whilst a variety of eight or fifteen day summer holiday destinations could be booked by calling at agents Dean and Dawsons in Eldon Street.

Several omnibuses can be seen on the town streets, though it was to be another ten years before a central

Above: Regent Street and the Congregational Church in the 1920s (*Elliott Collection*)

Above: The Wire Trellis Inn before its facelift. (*Tasker Collection*)

Above: Barnsley & District Motorbus, c.1926.
(*Yorkshire Traction Co*)

bus station was established on railway company land east of the viaduct — between Jumble Lane crossing and Exchange Station. The 1920s was a period of great expansion for the Barnsley and District Traction Company. By 1925 a fleet of 118 vehicles, all Leylands, operated a radiating network of services, peaking on market days. Competition was said to be so keen that drivers raced each other to the next stop, though the speed limit was supposed to be 12 m.p.h. From

Above: Jumble Lane Crossing and Exchange Station. (*Brian Hilton*)

November, 1928 the livery logos began changing to the Yorkshire Traction Company Limited and by the summer of 1930 the company's trams had gone.

From its 'planned' layout in the thirteenth century Barnsley developed a very compact form with the greatest density of properties found along and near Market Hill, Church Street and Westgate (Shambles Street). The aerial photograph certainly shows the narrow and congested nature of the early street pattern, though clearance of old properties had begun around the war memorial (1925) prior to the building of the new town hall and Technical College . After the First World War the new County Borough began responding to the government's advice to build 'Homes fit for Heroes' by developing municipal housing at the fringe of town, in areas such as Wilthorpe, Smithies, Kendray, Lundwood and Ardsley; and 1927 marked the start of a scheme to sweep away some of the crowded Victorian and Edwardian slums around the centre of town, re-housing tenants at Cundy Cross, Worsbrough Common, California Gardens and Burton Grange. Great change lay ahead but this aerial view provides us with an excellent starting point in our appreciation of the changing face of urban Barnsley.

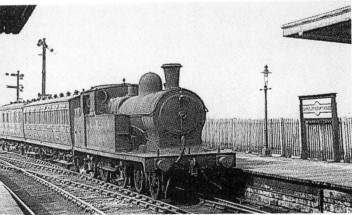

Above: Steam train arrives at Exchange Station. (*BMBC*)

Below: Unveiling of the War Memorial, 11 October, 1925, strategically placed as a centre piece for the future Town Hall building (see page 50).

The eighteenth century pedlar would have been pleased to see a small cluster of buildings huddled on Pinfold Hill, overlooking the final ascent into town following an arduous journey on foot, pack-saddled horse or on board a carrier's cart. The crossing of Barnsley Moor and the Race Common was relieved by the descent to Townend before entering the principal western thoroughfare where refreshments could be had at a convenient alehouse or inn, although some may have already stopped our traveller to buy stockings, a few buttons or thread 'for a bargain' before he reached market place or fairground. He may have had a regular tally-round of local calls to make, selling what he could, collecting a few coppers 'on account'; and then there was new stock to barter or buy before moving on.

From about 1800 lanes of varying importance converged at Townend radiating in four, five and eventually six directions — like spokes from the hub of a wheel. In the 1920s street-sellers such as the 'Paraffin Man' (a familiar figure with his horse and cartload,

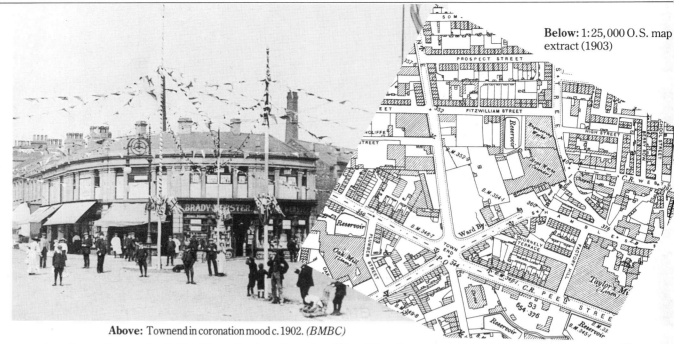

Below: 1:25,000 O.S. map extract (1903)

Above: Townend in coronation mood c. 1902. *(BMBC)*

emerging from the yard of the Mason's Arms) and Hawcock's mobile shop may have called for mutual business and a chat at wheelwright Daft and Norton's Peel Street yard.

Townend had not only become a central place of interest, with a character all its own but spaces between its emerging roads (as can be seen in Plate Two) had been infilled by a mix of mills, warehouses, engineering works and working class housing whilst small family businesses clung on either side of each arterial route, gradually thinning to an occasional corner or terrace shop the further away from town.

Like an aerial Lowry painting, it provides us with a striking image of our industrial past with small dark busily moving figures on apparently traffic-free streets.

The huge Hope Works dominates the lower western side of Sackville Street and Pinfold Hill. In 1928 the complex was shared by several concerns, including the Barnsley Cannister Company, which occupied the upper (Fitzwilliam Street) section containing the former top-lit sheds with their distinctive saw-tooth profile roofs, Broomhall's clothing company and S. Fletcher and Son's velvet works. The original mill (circa 1820) was re-built,

Above: Robert ('Paraffin Man') Strong. *(N. Gillott)*

Above: Part of the Hope Mill, Sackville Street   *(Tasker Collection)*

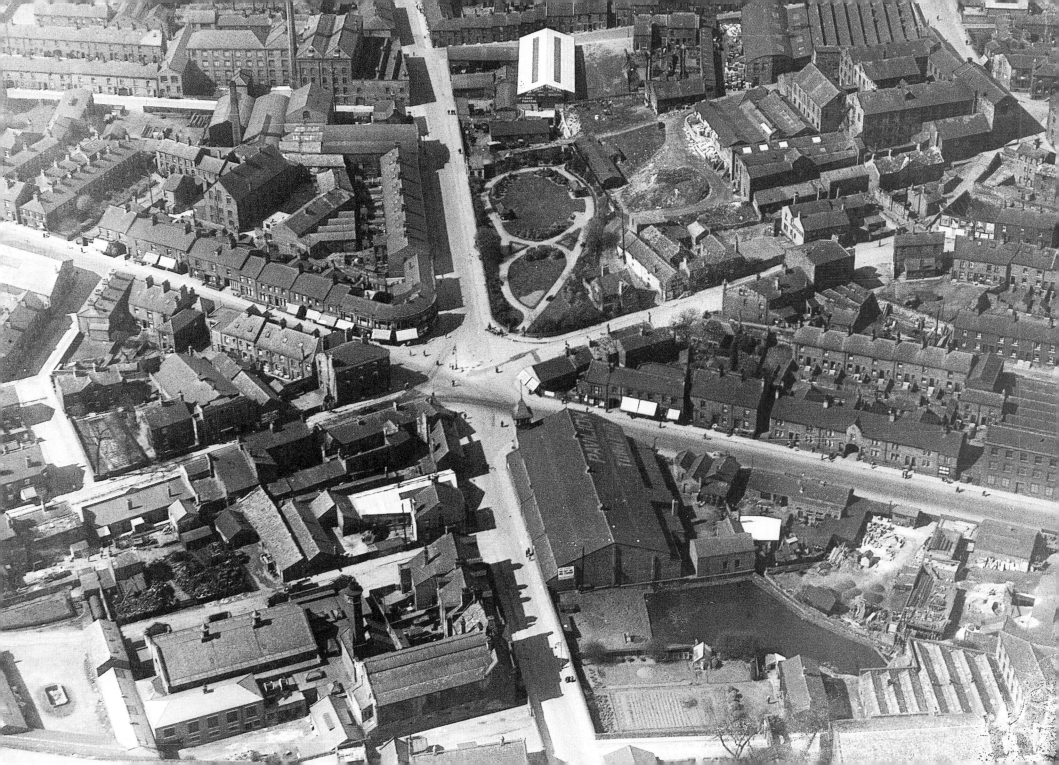

Above: The B.B.C.S. Peel Street branch.
(Elliott Collection)

Above: Townend Park and Fitzwilliam Street *(Elliott Collection)*

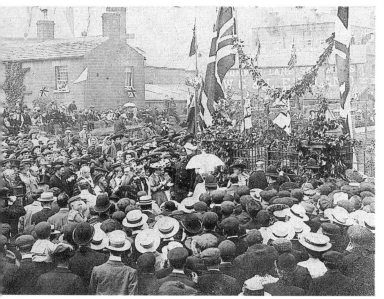

Above: The grand opening of Townend Recreation Ground, 1905
(Elliott Collection)

functioning as a steam-powered calender works where various types of linen cloth were 'finished'. By 1870 the Spencer brothers of Rob Royd House, Worsbrough Bridge, where their father had established a bleachworks, had developed a new printing process at Hope Mill, described in White's directory as 'extremely difficult, yet by great perseverance, and immense expense … had been brought to perfection'. For a few years prior to its closure the mill diversified into cotton spinning and weaving in addition to the printing of union cloth.

Though less commanding, part of the large premises of the Bore Spring Works, can be identified in the bottom right corner of the photograph. This linen mill was operated by Richardson, Tee and Rycroft until their removal to Redbrook Bleachworks in 1929. It is shown as a velvet works on the 1932 edition of the 1 : 2500 O.S. map, but was soon to be demolished to make way for the Ritz Cinema. The reservoir is the only survivor of at least five Townend 'ponds', mostly fed by the Sough Dike and each serving a linen mill. Before the adoption of gas or electricity a local water source was essential for both the raising of steam-power and the processing of linen. The white-roofed structure at the junction of Dodworth Road and Plumber Street, used as a garage between 1927-65 and then as R. Midgely's corn warehouse, occupies part of the former reservoir site of another old linen works: the Oak Mill which existed until at least 1906.

The back of a mostly single-storied building can be seen on Racecommon Road, opposite Plumber Street. This was originally part of another specialist textile building: the Hope Dyeworks, but was almost completely demolished in 1990. The last part of the important Taylor's Peel Street mill, an interesting structure of three storeys and five bays (which can be seen at the junction of Fenton Street) was demolished in 1991. Today none of the important pioneering

Above: Shambles Street from Townend *(Tasker Collection)*

Townend linen establishments have been preserved — a tremendous loss to Barnsley's industrial heritage.

There is a fine view of the south (Wharncliffe Street) side of the relatively modern Utilitas Works, its handsome main block rising between four to five storeys. It was established in 1867 by James McLintock who used an innovatory process in the making of down or quilt materials, said to give customers 'great warmth with little weight'. The brick structure has an unmistakable air of confidence. In the 1930s its ground floor was used for the dispatch of finished goods, the top for filling quilts and the other levels for the manufacture of quilts and dresses. Top rate of pay was thirty shillings (£1.50) per week but 'starters' only received seven shillings (35p). Payment, as at other mills, was by piece-work, a girl's 'rate' was dependent,

for example, by the number of seconds it took her to make a bedspread — for which she might have received 2½ (old) pence. Workers were subject to short-time in winter.

'McLintocks' overlooked the saw mill of W.G. & L. England and John Jackson's small 'Earl Cement & Buxton Lime' depot. The large warehouse facing Dodworth Road was the Newburgh Works, occupied by drysalters W.H. Jackson & Company. The industrial importance of Summer Lane is further emphasised by the distant view of the Qualter & Smith Brothers' engineering works where handsome iron lamp posts were cast, soon to be gaining the firm a national reputation, but initially made for Barnsley Corporation at a cost £3.50 in 1920's, a skilled man receiving £3.50 for a 47 hour week. A foundry had existed here from

at least 1822. Another saw mill, with a distinctive white roof, can be seen across from Utilitas, on lower Fitzwilliam Street. The adjacent arched-roofed building, at right-angles to Summer Lane and facing the mill, was one of Reynold Brothers' garages.

From the middle of the nineteenth century workers' housing began to appear near the mills, as landowners began to realise the financial attraction of their assets. The terrace was the main building form. It was low cost and could be erected with relative ease either in rows or back-to-back; and could even overcome the steep incline between Summer Lane and Sackville Street. Small enclosed courts lead from the backs of some terraces, a medieval style of building already common in nearby Shambles Street. It resulted in very crowded conditions, some rooms never receiving any daylight, an arrangement that had to be largely abandoned after Disraeli's great Public Health Act of 1875. Better quality small terraces, built between 1890 and 1908 emerged; and a good example can be seen facing Peel Street, divided by a central archway. The Co-operative grocery shop, with its blinds pulled down was conveniently only a few yards away. In contrast middle-class housing developed along parts of Sackville

Above: The former Masons Arms/Clarkson Brewery offices. *(Tasker Collection)*

Above: Many readers will have fond memories of 'Paramount Pictures' at the Pavilion Cinema which operated from 1920 to 1950 but it was previously used as the Olympic Skating Rink as can be seen by the adjoining illustration.

Above: The 'Olympic's' staff, band and expert skaters.

Street where some mill owners, such as James and Robert McLintock and John Henry Qualter preferred town 'villas' to country mansions so that they could 'keep an eye' on the works.

Life in a two-up and two down must have been hard for most people, but especially for women. Limited to one cold water tap, household chores such as cooking, cleaning and striving to keep away pervasive dirt had to be combined with managing on a very small budget. But there was great pride present, cleanliness a sign of status to the extent of using the 'donkey-stone' to decorate the front step. Despite hardship, terraced communities had some advantages. Often relatives and neighbours would look after children so that women could continue to work at the mill full-time.

For many ordinary people the idea of leisure in summer was to sit in a chair outside the front door and watch the world go by. Pubs such as the Wheatsheaf, Fitzwilliam and George and Dragon may have offered some relief for the working man, occasionally tempered by either tragic or comic scenes in the 'red-brick streets' on a Saturday night; but on the Lord's day morning it was a chance to put on your Sunday best, perhaps go to church or chapel or have a stroll with the family to Locke Park. Townend recreational ground, established on the site of the old Union Calender Mill, was opened amid great scenes of rejoicing in 1905, given to the town by Reverend Thornley Taylor, in memory of his father, Thomas Edward. But for increasing numbers of working class people, especially the younger generation, the most popular pastime was undoubtedly the silver screen which not only offered escapism but privacy for courting couples.

Entertainment at the popular Pavillion Cinema, where Paramount Pictures were first shown in Barnsley, was enlivened by means of music ('Everything from the latest Fox-Trot to the immortal works of Chopin, Beethoven [and], Wagner) from its 'Symphony Orchestra', under the direction of Mr G. Milton France.

Patrons could look forward to Esther Ralston in *Ten Modern Commandments*, Gary Cooper in *Arizona Bound* and Lon Chaney in *The Hunchback of Notre Dame*. This formidable landmark was originally built as the Olympia Skating Rink, in 1909 when roller skating was all the rage. Here, in July 1919 sports fans could see footage from America of 24 year old copper miner Jack Dempsey (The Manassa Mauler) pounding his way to the world heavyweight championship by overcoming the giant cowboy, Jess Willard in three awesome rounds. The Pavilion, fondly remembered by so many Barnsley people, was destroyed by fire in September, 1950. Nearby, in Racecommon Road, was the smaller Princess Picture Palace which offered Monday and Saturday matinees as well as evening performances. Soft drink sales probably sold well during the intermission of *Desert Dust*, starring 'super horseman' Ted Wells which also included 'hand-to-hand' fight scenes 'staged hundreds of feet in the air over rushing waters'.

A final word about recreation, and also education: the old (1874) and new (1914) Race Street Baths have for many years been distinctive buildings in this part of town, the smaller, assisted by its part grade II architectural status, even escaping demolition after the 1989 closure and more recently the construction of the Western Relief Road which has completely transformed Townend. The Baths were used by a variety of local organisations, including Barnsley Swimming Club (inaugurated in 1878) and the Barnsley Borough Police Swimming Club. Chief Constable Butler presided over the annual club breakfast at the Baths in 1920. Part of the rooftop of St George's School can just be seen a few yards south of the old Baths. In 1927 the school could accommodate up to 306 girls, Miss Agnes Whitelock being the mistress in charge.

PAVILION
BARNSLEY.
WEEK COMMENCING MONDAY, MAY 7th.

MONDAY, TUESDAY & WEDNESDAY.
ESTHER RALSTON
with NEIL HAMILTON in
10 MODERN COMMANDMENTS
litely sermon in new ideas, with the beauti-
ul Star of "Sons of the Sea" in another of
entrancing roles.

SHORT TAILS   WHEN WE WERE KIDS
(2 Reel Comedy).   (Pictorial Poetry).
PATHE PICTORIAL   PATHE SUPER GAZETTE
the Best Magazine).   (Greatest News Film).

BIG WEEK-END PROGRAMME.
THURSDAY, FRIDAY & SATURDAY.
TWO STAR ATTRACTIONS!
GARY COOPER in
ARIZONA BOUND
Easy-come and Easy-go Harper, trotting the
trail that leads to thrills and high adventure.
Drama of the quick-gun sort!
RAYMOND GRIFFITH,
THE IMMACULATE JOKER, in
WEDDING BILLS
RAY in another of his delightful Comedies of
a Thousand Errors.
EVE'S FILM REVIEW,   SUPER GAZETTE,
The Ladies' Favourite.   The Big News Reel.

SUPERB MUSIC BY THE PAVILION SYMPHONY ORCHESTRA.
Everything from the latest Fox-Trot to the immortal works of Chopin, Beethoven, Wagner.

MAY 14TH. LON CHANEY IN THE HUNCHBACK OF NOTRE DAME.
Coming Shortly: "THE STREET OF FORGOTTEN MEN," with PERCY MARMONT,
and EMIL JANNINGS in "THE WAY OF ALL FLESH."
The Sign That Ensures The Show!
Pavilion Paramount Pictures   1757

Above: Entertaining Barnsley folk at the 'Pav' on the week of the aerial sortie were **Top:** The hugely popular Lon Chaney, in the *Hunchback of Notre Dame*; **Centre:** Raymond Griffith in *Wedding Bells*; **Bottom:** A young Gary Cooper, soon to become a movie legend.

Right: Samuel Marsland, Barnsley Police Swimming Instructor, who taught at the Public Baths. He is obviously proud of his custom-made costume, with float-action bags (on his hips) and, star and fleur-de-lys designs.

Plate Three provides us with a superb aerial view of Taylor's Mill, Barnsley's most extensive linen factory, which can be seen dominating the north side of Peel Street and partly extending back to Shambles Street. Rows of low weaving sheds contrast with the multi-storied mill buildings and great chimney, blackened by decades of smoke and grime, but already a redundant monument of another age. The steam-powered mill was opened in 1845 by Edward Taylor, fourth generation of a family of Barnsley linen manufacturers and was much enlarged afterwards. By 1900 local mills tended to concentrate on near luxury products in the wake of the slow decline in trade. Listed as 'Thomas Taylor & Sons (Barnsley) Ltd' in a textile directory of 1919-20, the mill then made 'fancy drills, vestings, damask etc' and had 1,000 twist spindles and 430 looms. Taylors' continued in business for a few more years, processing cotton cloth from their Manchester mill but by 1931 the former weaving sheds had been taken over by the Yorkshire Tyre Rubber Company.

Reference to the crowded upper right quarter of the photograph gives us a distant view of a fascinating area of workers' cottages and the occasional detached property, lost in recent years through slum clearance and redevelopment. Westgate was connected to Churchfield by four streets: Berry Row, School Street, North Pavement and Roper Street, whilst High Street enclosed a corner of Sackville Street. Many of the cottages here, some (like Collier Row, arranged in short terraces, others in enclosed courts identified only by a number) had been occupied by mill workers and miners since mid-Victorian times.

High Field House, in Sackville Street (opposite Fitzwilliam Street), is just in view and was one of the 'better' properties. It served as the private residence and office of removal contractor T. Master Ltd. The Black Boy Inn (in School Street), hosted by Ernest Walker, was one of the workers' 'locals'. Several important public buildings can be identified. We get a glimpse from Westgate of the south facade of St Mary's Boys' School which functioned from 1911-67. With its

Above: 1:25,000 O.S. map extract (1903).

entrance facing Churchfield and extending along the west side of Roper Street we have a view of the town fire engine (and later ambulance) garage. Near the eastern end and north side of Westgate is the County Police Station where superintendent Wilfred Blacker supervised three inspectors, thirteen sergeants, one detective sergeant and a force of ninety-four constables. Next door, and just in shot, the Court House of 1879 which extended along part of St Mary's Gate. The tall building almost opposite the police station was a warehouse; but until loosing its licence in 1908 was the Empire Palace, earlier known as the Surrey Music Hall.

Much of the land between Shambles Street and

Above: Taylor's Mill, Peel Street. *(Tasker Collection)*

Above: Steam-roller on Peel Street. *(Dennis Gill)*

streets were named after prominent statesman and military figures: Pitt, Nelson, Blücher, Castlereagh (out of view) and Wellington. Here workers' houses mingle between and behind small businesses and the occasional 'public' building. Chennel's Bars and the Corner Pin offered a choice for drinkers at the end of Wellington Street, though the Imperial Hotel of 1905, with its ornate tower was just round the corner facing Peel Square. Our bird's eye view allows us to appreciate the size and importance of the Theatre Royal by reference to its ascending roof-top. Some Barnsley people may recall seeing variety entertainers such as George Formby Senior, Frank Randall, Arthur Haynes and Charlie Chester perform at the Royal. The present grade II listed building, erected at a cost of £16,000 in 1898, was designed by Walter Emden, the London architect responsible for the famous Garrick Theatre. According to Kelly's Directory of 1927 the Theatre Royal and Opera House, owned by a limited company and managed by Mr A. C. Mitchell, 'had a stage of ample dimensions' and was 'fully equipped with all

Westgate consisted of small yards and courts set amid cramped dwellings which had been successively renewed since late medieval times. We know from deeds that properties here were leased to one or (usually) several individuals/families, reverting back to the owner after a specified time. The aerial photograph and map provides us with a valuable record of this very crowded mixture of inns and houses, so soon to vanish without trace. Speaking of disappearing buildings, the large white-roofed structure in Westgate, with gabled porch

was a magnificent timber-framed aisled 'tithe barn' of six bays, partly converted for use as a butcher's shop. Probably late medieval, it was certainly of architectural interest but 'dismantled' in c.1964 and never re-built. Timbers were inexcusably dumped on council-owned open ground with inevitable deterioration and subsequent loss, making a mockery of tentative plans for reconstruction on another site.

Another interesting and typically congested area of town can be seen at the bottom of the photograph where

Above: Dismantling the Westgate barn. *(BMBC)*

necessary appliances in case of fire' (it was originally gas-lit) and could seat 2,000 persons. On the evening of 8 May, 1928, the day our aerial photograph was taken, Miss Pauline Drake and the Imperial Players were performing in the comedy *Patty*, the story of a London Cockney flower girl. There is now considerable public interest in the restoration and re-opening of 'The Royal', guided by a steering committee of the Theatre Royal Trust.

At the corner of Blucher Street and Peel Street was the Albion Inn, associated with the Leatham family from 1880 to 1933. Across the street the back of the National School can be seen, also known as the Ellis or Free School after the charity founded by George Ellis of Brampton in his will of 1711. Built by trustees and subscriptions in 1813, the school was taken over by St George's church in 1867. Sixty years later it catered for 241 boys, Herbert Holling being master. This interesting building, with its elegant facade, was

Below: National (Ellis) School, Pitt Street. *(Tasker Collection)*

Above: One-room house, Blucher Street. *(BMBC)*

demolished in 1963. Nearby, in Nelson Street, part of Holy Rood (Roman Catholic) School is also in view. It had places for 494 boys and girls. Mr James Sinclair was master, Miss Ellen Braxton mistress whilst Miss Julia Sullivan had charge of 224 infants.

The churches of St Georges' and Holy Rood which opened for worship in 1822 and 1905 respectively, and their associated day and Sunday schools, helped meet some of the social and educational needs of many families in and around this area; but others preferred attendance at one of several non-conformist chapels present in the photograph. The Primitive Methodists assembled in the early Georgian building which can be seen occupying a commanding position at the end of Westgate, later (1947-50) adapted for the use of the Barnsley Boys' Club, and now a listed building.

We get an even better view of the great Wesleyan church in Pitt Street. Built in 1845/46 to the design of James Simpson, it was closed for services in may 1982 because of high maintenance costs. In the apparent absence of an interested purchaser, and despite widespread recognition of its considerable architectural

Above: Workers' houses, Blucher Street. *(BMBC)*

merit, demolition followed almost two years later. A more modest chapel, dating from 1829 but given a face-lift 1901 can be seen in Blucher Street. Here, in 1928 the United Methodists were celebrating alterations and the installation of a new organ.

Although less imposing than its Wesleyan neighbour the Temperance Hall has escaped demolition, though not alteration, and has a varied and colourful history. Completed in 1837, when Princess Victoria became Queen, it was commissioned by the 'Oddfellows', a fraternal organisation similar to the Freemasons; but by 1850 the Pitt Street building had been converted by Thomas Dale as a 'Furnishing Warehouse' when it was advertised as 'The Mart', and then, in deference to its Grecian facade as 'The Atheneum'.

From 1880-1897 the hall was used by the Barnsley Temperance Society. Following service as a private school it was transformed into a cinema and from 1923-28 was known as The Cosy Picture House. It subsequently housed the Central School of Dancing before reverting back to a warehouse under the occupancy of J. W. Farnsworth.

As recently as the 1960s Pitt Street was described as 'The best street in Barnsley' by the architectural historian Sir Nicholas Pevsner but very few buildings that once caught the eye now remain. Part of the fine later Georgian facade of St George's Place, for example, can be seen in front of Bore Spring Mill. It was pulled down in 1937. One of the most distinctive buildings to survive stands where Pitt Street meets Wellington Street and overlooks Peel Square. 'Chronicle Buildings' had been the home of *The Barnsley Chronicle* since 1878 and was the focus of large patriotic crowds when general election results were announced. Under the guidance of Sir Joseph Hewitt, grandfather of the present owners, the newspaper quickly outshone local competitors, and by 1930 was established, with new works, at its present Church Street site. The handsome Peel Square building has housed a variety of concerns over the years but in 1957 became the premises of the

Right: Row of cottages by the Vine Tavern, Pitt Street. *(Tasker Collection)*

Left: Dale's Furnishing Warehouse (from a Victorian advert).

Below: Edwardian Pitt Street. *(Elliott Collection)*

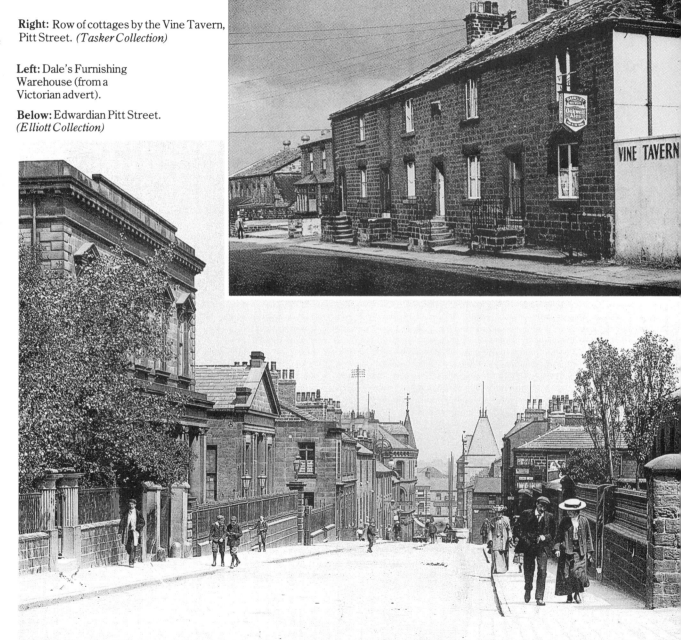

Above: Peel Square in about 1910. *(Elliott Collection)*

Above: The 'Paraffin Man' enters Peel Street. *(N. Gillott)*

Above: 'Stage Coach', Peel Square. *(Dennis Gill)*

York County (later TSB) Savings Bank. It is now a Tetley public house.

By the 1920s the motorised taxi had replaced the horse-drawn cab and examples can be seen awaiting custom in their traditional Peel Square location, in front of the White Hart Hotel, where Thomas Elstone was licensee. The few businesses capable of buying a modern commercial vehicle might call at Reynolds Brothers' Peel Street garage (whose rooftop is in view behind the Weslayan church and opposite Taylor's mill), where the latest Dodge van was available for £285. There is also a good view of the rear of the King George Hotel standing next to the former three-storey corn mill,

which from 1927 was occupied by another emerging motor concern: Eyre Brothers Ltd, noted for its Austin sales and service, on this site until 1967.

In the middle right of the photograph, between Graham's Orchard (formerly Wilson Street) and the ancient footpath/passageway known as Dog Lane we can look down on an elegant house with one of its two projecting end bays just visible. This was probably the first considerable brick residence to be built in Barnsley, appropriately known as Red House. In late Georgian times the old market town was being transformed under the stimulus of the developing linen industry. There was a demand for houses in town near to the new

workplaces, but space was limited. Cesspits competed with wells in the increasingly unhealthy backyards of Shambles Street. However, here we have an exception: a small 'country' residence in the middle of the town. But when Red House was built Peel Street had not developed, so its owner, Quaker entrepeneur John Wilson, enjoyed an interrupted prospect towards Peashills from his south-facing garden which sloped down to the unculvated Sough Dyke. The rural rich would not have contemplated purchasing a town property, let alone build a new house, but for some new industrialists a grand town house could not only be convenient but also a symbol of success. Paradoxically, Wilson's somewhat eccentric younger brother, William, whose lucrative enterprises were copied by subsequent linen pioneers, preferred to live in a dilapidated house off Church Street.

Above: Red House. *(Tasker Collection)*

Shambles Street, formerly known as Westgate, can be seen junctioning with Sackville Street in the upper middle part of the aerial view. Here traffic traditionally diverged westwards towards Huddersfield or proceeded southwards via the Race Common. Not surprisingly many inns developed on either side of the main thoroughfare into town. Among the lost ones were the Globe, Wellington, Horns, Black Bull, Three Crowns, Glass Lantern, Cock, Sovereign, Windmill and White Horse/Fleece. Those surviving in 1928 on the north

Left: Shambles Street before road widening. *(Dennis Gill)*

Right: Samuel Marsland and his young bakery staff. *(Paul Midwood)*

side were the white-fronted and two-storey Old White Bear, one of Barnsley's most ancient hostelries. The gabled building about four properties below the 'Bear', after Surrey Yard, was the Musical Tavern (formerly Beehive Inn) whilst the interesting Old Windmill Hotel by Rich Lane, and the more modern Stores Inn, vied for trade near the Sackville junction. On the south side of the street the substantial rear of the late Victorian Lord Nelson Hotel, is easily seen, dominating the head of Graham's Orchard whilst at the west side of the top of Dog Lane is the rooftop of the Three Travellers, the only 'original' Shambles Street inn to survive to the present day. Change is inevitable but for an entire historic town street to be decimated of so much character remains one of the great tragedies of modern Barnsley.

Above: Part of Shambles Street from a site closed for development, the distinctive Three Travellers Inn in view. *(BMBC)*

Right: The Barnsley Steam Bakery (Marslands), 37 Shambles Street. *(Paul Midwood)*

Smoke pours out of the great brick chimney and steam escapes from the roof of the Yorkshire Paper Mill, an agglomeration of buildings sandwiched between the river Dearne and the Aire & Calder Navigation (Barnsley Canal). A small group of barges, moored in Old Mill basin, await to be relieved of their loads of Finish wood-pulp. A boatload of about 60 tons might consist of 300 bales of compressed pulp, which had to be hoisted and stacked in neat piles in the mill yard by means of three steam-powered jib-cranes which can be seen stationed along the wharfside. Bales were fed into the beaterhouse where the pulp was broken up and dispersed by machine, a process known as beating or refining.

In May 1928 the new mill manager was Dubliner Mr George P. Fleming who spoke of 'a bright future for the Barnsley Mills' but he was soon replaced by W.J. Chappell of London.

On a December morning in 1928 'two nervous boys' stood inside the fitting shop door of the paper mill, waiting to be told 'where to go and what to do' at the start of their first day at work. "Thee, go ovver thear to that door. Tell 'em I've sent thee. Th'all be an electrician's apprentice. Thee get thissen a brush and start sweeping t'shop up. Th'all be a fitter's apprentice". So were two lives mapped out, as remembered by Walter Ridley who started his working life with a brush in his hands at the age of fourteen years and two days.

Left: Old Mill photographed from Eldon Street North in 1973. *(Brian Elliott)*

Apprentices, as in other industries, were often too expensive to keep on when they had completed their term. Walter felt fortunate at getting work at the sister Blackburn mill but he eventually returned to Barnsley.

Before 1945 the mill concentrated on the production of quality note and printing papers by means of up to five machines: two Fourdriniers and two 'M.G.' machines in the main 'Top-side' mill and another Fourdrinier in the almost self-contained 'Low-side' mill (furthest away from the camera). At the wet end of the process slushed pulp of beaten fibres flowed on a moving band of fine wire mesh; and there, aided by suction, much of the water was drained away, leaving fibres and most of the additives resting on top. The wet 'web' of paper moved to the press section where it was carried on felt and passed between rollers that

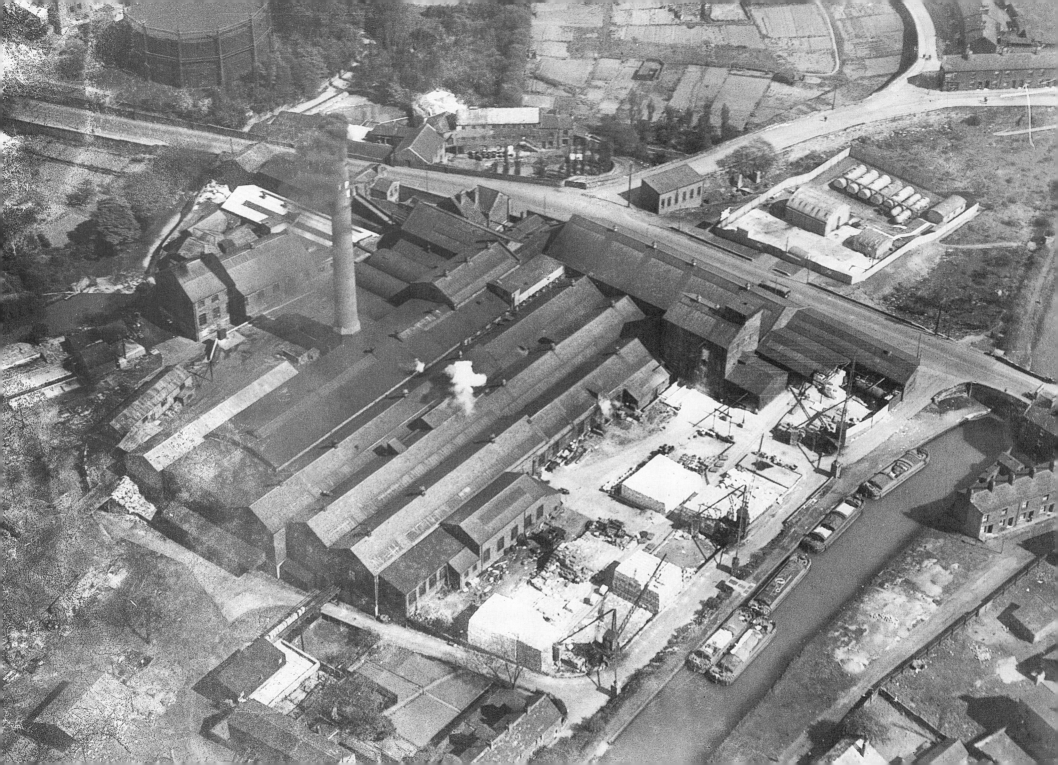

removed more water. The web, now much drier, was transferred on to another felt surface in passing over numerous drying cylinders. The material was given its final finish at the end of the process when it passed through numerous calendering rollers. Mrs Gladys Turton (nee Wingell), born in 1900, remembered that during the First World War young girls like herself had the job of 'jumping into a pit under the machines whilst they were still working' to assist with the flow of paper. Apart from the highly dangerous nature of the work (she once got her arm caught) it also involved the lifting of heavy materials. Working from 6 am until 5 pm, Gladys got 7s.6d. (37½p) per week. Her husband, now aged 98, worked at the Old Mill gasworks. Unless needing special treatment, the completed paper was then ready for storage and dispatch, either by rail (from the nearby Old Mill Goods Yard) or via company-owned or contracted road vehicles. James Enoch, who had horses stabled at Old Mill wharf, did some of the local carting between mill and railway.

We know from the memories of 'horse marines' such as Herbert Rogerson of Crofton whose family hired

Above: A barge being loaded with petroleum, Old Mill Basin. *(Alan Hall Collection)*

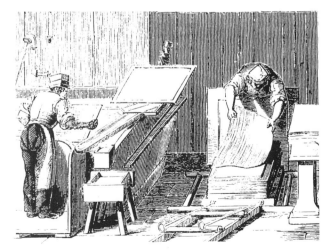

Above: Hand-made paper making.

horses and men to the boat owners, that the wood-pulp began its long journey from Finland to Humberside. The cargo was discharged from ship to barges in one of Hull's docks and then hauled in convoy behind a steam tug up the Humber and Ouse to Goole where a smaller tug completed the journey to Wakefield. If all went well some of the barges would arrive in Barnsley by late afternoon of the third day, towed by horses. The men had then to return overland to Wakefield, perhaps after refreshment at the Keel Inn, which can be seen in the bottom right of Plate Four. The five barges in view would have completed the final part of their journey by passing under Old Mill Bridge via Barnsley Basin and Barnsley Aqueduct (not in view). The boats may then have been turned around in Honeywell Basin (not in view), a few yards below the Keel Inn. But the five vessels were probably the remains of a larger convoy. Large barges could only travel as far as Heath Lock so their loads were transferred by the Rogersons to smaller vessels which had returned empty from Barnsley. These would then deliver another quantity of pulp to the mill, some of them returning with sixty or seventy tons of Barnsley coal.

The mill also needed considerable supplies of coal,

at about fifteen shillings per delivered ton, particularly to meet the needs of steam turbines 'Nancy' and 'Mary' (named after Marsden's daughters) in the main works and 'Little Nipper' in the Low-side mill. The main engines 'gleamed and shone due to the attention given by the enginemen', recalled Mr Ridley who was initially 'quite nervous at first going near them' due to their huge dimensions.

Walter Rogerson (no relation to Herbert) came to Barnsley in 1927 to assist his father who was contracted to convey 30,000 tons of coal a year to the paper mills, collected from colliery staithes on the Barnsley Canal and from Barnsley Main via a short stretch of the Dearne and Dove. The Rogersons had eight 61 foot wooden barges for this purpose and kept a horse at the Keel Inn whose stables are just visible. Coal was off-loaded on to railway wagons and shunted by an engine to the front of the boilers. The mill began using cheaper opencast coal in 1941 so waterborne deliveries ceased. The Rogerson business survived for a few more years by delivering pit coal from Wharncliffe Woodmoor to Redfearns glassworks wharf. Shortly before the closure of the canal some of Mr Rogerson's barges were marooned at Smithies but in 1984 four were 'rescued' from the silt and mud, along with numerous artifacts, by a team of Manpower Service Commission workers and Barnsley Canal Group volunteers.

The chute which can be seen connecting the roadside buildings of the Low Mill was probably for the transfer of rags from the more distant building. Cyril Walton, born 1909, recalled how 'Dolly', his elder sister, worked here as a rag sorter — and doubled as a crane driver in the Great War.

An enormous amount of water was required so as to ensure the mill's continuous operation. The level of the Fleets Dam was maintained by means of a pumping station which took water from the Dearne. Effluent from

Above: Old Mill Lane Bridge, Aire & Calder Navigation (Barnsley Canal) and Canal Street, winter 1953-54. *(BMBC)*

the machines was pumped into the multi-coloured river, mostly at night. Torrential rain in the summer of 1932 resulted in the river and dam overflowing causing great damage to the Low Mill, evacuation by boat of cottages near the Tollgate Hotel (Bentleys) and flooding of the main road. Subsequently Barnsley Corporation widened and improved Wakefield Road and built a new bridge, which opened in 1936.

Despite the apparent activity in Plate Four all was not well in the mid-1920s, at least with regard to the mill management and ownership. The company's affairs passed to the specially formed Dearne Paper Works Ltd in 1924 but its speculative shareholders, mostly Oxford undergraduates, could not raise sufficient capital to purchase the mill which remained in the hands of creditors. A year later Charles Diamond, proprietor of The Catholic Herald, founded Yorkshire Paper Mills Ltd but also found that the company shares did not sell well; and trading was undermined by profits not large enough to cover external loans. Not surprisingly, as the depression worsened, the company made a loss of £20,000 in 1926, the year of the miners' strike but struggled on until the severe winter of 1929 when frozen waterways badly affected trade in northern Europe. The price of pulp and cellulose rose so high that production, consisting of 16,000 tons (per annum) of printing paper, newsprint and notepaper had become unprofitable. Mr Ridley recalled how workpeople of varying ranks were dispatched to neighbouring newspaper offices 'begging them not to cancel their orders'. The company ceased trading in November 1931. The mill, its site and relatively modern equipment was purchased by Star Paper Ltd for £55,000, a modest figure which reflected its troubled recent history and the worsening economy. The new, Blackburn-based owners, a subsidiary of Kymmene Aktiebolag of Helsinki, concentrated on the production of high quality

Above: Gladys Wingell, with her shawl, on her way to work at the mill. *(A.D. Turton)*

printing and packing paper at the Barnsley site. The rescue meant that wood pulps were exclusively supplied and shipped by the parent company which had both Britons and Finns as directors.

The mill went on to play a small part in helping the British bomber offensive against Nazi Germany. We know from the papers of the late Mr Harold Brooke who worked as a cost clerk from 1928-71 that top-secret work by select employees under the supervision of A.J. Blake concerned the manufacture of aluminium-coated strips which were dropped by 'pathfinder' planes to fox German radar.

In 1979 the Star Paper Group had a turnover of £49 million (from a production of 110,986 tonnes) and profits, after depreciation, of over £1 million. But the mill closed somewhat abruptly on 14 August 1981, after fifty years of almost continuous production, when the remaining 250 workers came off the night shift and were given an extended paid holiday. This historic industrial site is now occupied by the Asda supermarket and McDonald's fast-food restaurant.

Large-scale mechanised paper manufacturing had in fact begun on the site in 1867 when the Sheffield firm of Charles Marsden & Sons took over the Dearne works, later known as the Lower Mill (to distinguish it from the Valley Mill at Smithies, also to be Marsden-owned) which had been almost totally destroyed by fire. Under the direction of Thomas Marsden the new business prospered. He employed 600-700 hands, according to the census of 1881, with occupational titles such as 'rag [and old rope] sorter, rag picker, rag chopper, paper sorter, folder, calenderer, engineman, stoker, carter and warehouseman'. Thomas Marsden, of a Derbyshire family, also owned the Winter Colliery at Smithies and resided, rather grandly, at Cliffe House, Monk Bretton. During the summer months he rented the more commodious Banks Hall at Cawthorne, and it was whilst

Above: George Kilner, mill chauffeur for over 45 years. *(J. Tongue)*

there that he died in 1893. He had been very active in public life and served as Mayor of Barnsley between 1886-88 and, according to his obituarist, 'never had any disputes with his workpeople'.

Some accommodation was provided for employees and their families within the mill yard. One of the properties in the terrace of three houses known as Dearne Villas (end on to the pulp stacks in the aerial photograph) was occupied by Mr George Kilner and his young family from the early 1930s. Mr Kilner (1905-1971) who worked as chauffer for the manager, started at the paper mill in about 1922.

This particular part of the Dearne Valley had been an attractive industrial location well before the canal was built; small water-powered enterprises associated with iron and wool having been established by the Benedictine monks of Monk Bretton in late medieval times. Disputes concerning the relative use of water between the 'iron mills' and corn mills were the subject of litigation in the Tudor period. Hand-made papermaking appears to have been present at Smithies from at least the 1660s, its 'art and mystery' passing down the generations, notably via the Rhodes family, until about 1780. In the 1740s linen pioneer William Wilson had established a bleachcroft by the side of the Dearne, where there was a plentiful supply of water from both the river and nearby Honeywell spring. Wilson's enterprising nephew, Joseph Beckett,

Above: Barnsley Canal (with sunken barge) and the Keel Inn c1970. (*Brian Elliott*)

where he would stay overnight. Liverpool had five hide and skin markets supplied by a wide area including Wales and Ireland. Mr Barker's business was by no means over, for he then journeyed to Manchester, ordering more skins and, not surprisingly, returned home feeling very tired. Small quantities of skins were occasionally obtained from contracts in Doncaster, Leicester and Nottingham. Well-known local hauliers Joe Cutts and Son of Vernon Street were used for the deliveries. Yard foreman George Bithell, who lived at 1, Twibell Street, was often called upon to supervise and assist the unloading of the skins. George, of Welsh origin, came to Old Mill from Bootle after completing his apprenticeship 'in the art of fellmongering' in 1889. A key worker, his daughters told the writer how the occasional fox skin was taken in for 'curing' during the fashionable twenties.

Fellmongering had changed little since medieval times. It was, in the words of Mr Moody, 'a very crude industry . . . a smelly and mucky job'. Dirt, salt, bloodclots etc, were removed or loosened by soaking

Below: The Old Mill 'Tannery', June 1977 (*Jim Badics*)

regarded as 'father' of the local linen trade, soon began 'manufacturing' nearby. By the 1820s Russell and Company were operating as 'flax spinners' but, according to recent research by Tanya Schmoller, the site also appears to have been used as a small scale paper mill under the direction of the Watsons.

The premises of another traditional but largely forgotten industry can be seen opposite the paper mill, between the gas works and Harborough Hill Road. Robert Barker & Son, a small family concern, operated here as fellmongers (dealers in skins) — although the site is marked as 'Tannery' on contemporary large-scale maps. The firm was located at Old Mill in 1849 by a tanner, Robert Barker of Otley (a noted leather centre)

who appears to have soon converted to dealing in sheep skins than processing hides. Mr Norman Moody, great-grandson of its founder, took over the business from his uncle, Robert Barker II, in 1950, having worked in the yard from 1931. The Northern Butchers' Hide and Skin Company of Bailey Street (Sheffield Road) delivered 'fresh' sheep skins from local farms and slaughter houses, accounting for about 80 per cent of supplies. Salted skins had to be obtained from more distant sources.

Mr Moody recalled his uncle travelling to the hide and skin market in Leeds on Thursdays, then calling at Bradford Wool Exchange (to make deals with wool merchants), and moving on to Liverpool in the evening

This Indenture

This Indenture Witnesseth that *George Bithele*

doth put h**im**self APPRENTICE to *William Catlewgh Jones*

to learn h**is** Art, and with h**im** (after the manner of an Apprentice) to serve from the *12th* day of *July 1889.* unto the full end and term of *Seven Years* from thence next following, to be fully complete and ended: DURING which Term the said Apprentice h**is** M**aster** faithfully shall serve, h**is** secrets keep, h**is** lawful commands everywhere gladly do. Shall do no damage to h**is** M**aster** nor see to be done of others, but to h**is** power shall let or forthwith give warning to h**is** said M**aster** of the same. Shall not waste the Goods of h**is** said M**aster** nor lend them unlawfully to any. Shall not do any act whereby h**is** said M**aster** may have any loss with h**is** own goods or others during the said Term, without Licence of h**is** said M**aster.** Shall neither buy nor sell, nor absent h**im**self from h**is** said M**aster's** service day or night unlawfully; but in all things as a faithful Apprentice shall behave h**im**self towards h**is** said M**aster** and all h**is** during the said Term. And the said *William Catlewgh Jones*

h**is** said Apprentice in the Art of *Fellmongering* which he use**s** by the best means that /he can, shall teach and instruct, or cause to be taught and instructed, *paying the said apprentice* ~~finding unto the said Apprentice sufficient Meat, Drink,~~ ~~Lodging, and all other necessaries during the said Term~~ *Six Shillings per week for 1st & 2nd Year. 7/- Per week, for 3 & 4th Year and 8/- per week for remainder of his apprenticeship*

And for the true performance of all and every the said Covenants and Agreements, either of the said Parties bindeth h**im**self unto the other by these Presents **In Witness** whereof the Parties above named have hereunto set their hands and Seals the *12th day* Day of *July* in the Year of our Lord One Thousand Eight Hundred *Eighty nine*

Signed, Sealed, and Delivered by the above named

George Bithell

W C Jones   *Sarah Bithell*

Sold by [...] Co. [...] Fleet Street, E.C.

Left: Apprenticeship Indenture of George Bithell, 12 July 1889. *(M. Hill)*

Left: 'Fatty' Green, Walter Ferry (standing) and George Bithell. *(M. Hill)*

Right: One of Cutts' lorries loaded with bottles in sacks. Denton Street Garage, 1930s. The Redfearns logo was painted on the vehicle because Cutts' transported bottles for them on a regular basis. The haulage business started in about 1910 when horses pulled barges on the canal. *(Joe Cutts & Son)*

the skins overnight in pits of water fed by the Sough Dyke. The skins were then removed by hand and stacked on rails to drain. About eight labourers were involved in this heavy work. In order to 'burn' off the hair roots from the flesh side of the skins sodium sulphide and lime were brushed on. On the next day the skins were carried 'over the shoulder' across the yard and up numerous steps to the 'pulling shop' where three or four skilled men removed and sorted the wool into baskets according to quality. The wool was dried by means of stoves using coke from the adjacent gasworks – an extremely hot job.

The pelts were sold nationwide to leather-dressers, chiefly for the production of soft 'shammys', but also for bookbinding, handbags and suchlike. There was also a European market, for pelts were packed in ex-Co-operative Society jam casks, sealed by a Barnsley Brewery cooper and shipped to Antwerp for the National Tannery of Belgium: an interesting example of Barnsley ingenuity and enterprise. In 1960 the business became part of the Fatstock Marketing Corporation but continued to be managed by Mr Moody until the site

was closed down in 1967, a large fellmongery having been bought at Meanwood, Leeds. The old buildings remained in a state of dereliction until the late 1970s when the site was levelled and replaced by the present MFI store.

The terraced rows of houses partly in view in Canal Street, in Harborough Hill Road (where Mrs Joanna Bywater kept the corner shop) and Twibell Street were occupied mainly by workers from the papermill, gasworks (inaugurated 3 October, 1870) and Redfearns glassworks. The enclosure containing cylinders, opposite the mill, was a BP petroleum depot and the adjacent building an electricity sub-station, later converted into a joiner/undertaker's workshop.

It is perhaps fitting to leave one of the most historic areas of Barnsley by reference to a few lines from the former poet and town postmaster, Thomas Lister, who was born at Old Mill in 1810:

> *Lo! o'er Dearne's stream that gently slides,*
> *Bleak Barnsley's cloud-wreathed head,*
> *Where trade, not kind to all, provides*
> *Her children's well-earned bread.*

Miners were in the middle of their bitter dispute with the Conservative Government of Stanley Baldwin, more than two months after the end of the General Strike, and Rudolf Valentino had just completed what was to be his last film, *Son of the Sheik* when an aerial view of part of Stairfoot was taken, on Wednesday 14 July, 1926. For most of us the only easily recognisable feature is Grange Lane (across the upper part of the photograph) which joined the main road to Pontefract at Cundy Cross. The Talbot almshouses (erected in 1658), which survived until about 1950, are just discernable next to the taller 'Abbey Mill' ('Mill of the Black Monks' public house) in the extreme left-hand corner of the photograph, whilst almost opposite stands Burton Grange and the site of Monk Bretton Priory. Four existing streets of late Victorian terraced properties: Foster, Conway, Victoria and Hopewell, form short but distinctive terraces between Hoyle Mill Road (which becomes Oaks Lane as it passes the glassworks) and a patchwork of allotment gardens.

The camera was aimed at the premises of the Rylands Glass and Engineering Company which can be seen straddling the Dearne and Dove Canal surrounded by a complex network of railways. Viewed from above its appearance and layout is little different to that of other factories. The new Victorian glasshouses were far more anonymous landscape features than their predecessors. There was no need for the striking conical brick structures which served as both chimney and workplace for earlier generations. Instead we can see rows of sheds housing furnaces and workshops and a pair of typical factory chimneys. Shortly after the First World War new machinery was installed and the 'white' appearance of the modern looking sheds suggests that a considerable amount of capital investment had recently taken place. Despite this, production problems, labour disputes and declining sales of an increasingly obsolete

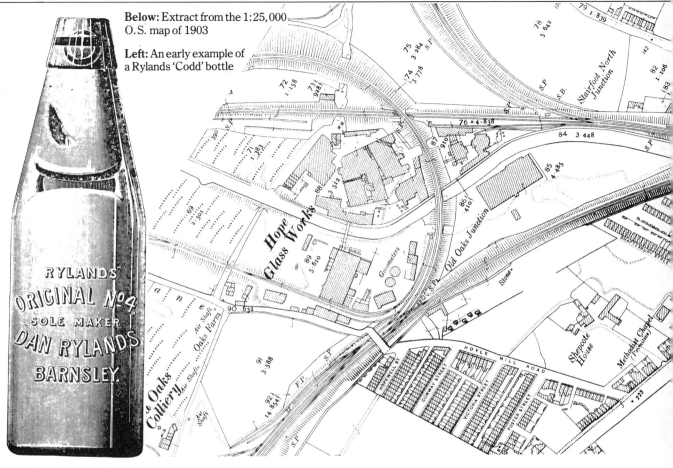

Below: Extract from the 1:25,000 O.S. map of 1903

Left: An early example of a Rylands 'Codd' bottle

product lead to the closure of the factory within a few months of this early flight.

The works were established here by Benjamin Rylands in 1867 principally for the production of bottles at a time, as Denis Ashurst has shown, was a remarkably busy period for the south Yorkshire glass industry. In Barnsley Redfearns had only recently developed their bottle and container works at Old Mill and by 1870 Wood Brothers' flint glass works transferred from Worsbrough to Hoyle Mill. Rylands arrived at Stairfoot with considerable business experience at the old Don

(Mexborough) and Swinton glassworks. The adoption of the name of The Hope Glass Works may have been in keeping with his ambitions but also occurred at a time when workers in almost every occupation lived in fear of losing their jobs and, as we shall see, there was an air of gloom over the locality.

A canalside location with plenty of space for expansion was an obvious attraction. Silican, in the form of fine sand, the basic but bulky raw material for glassmaking could be delivered by barge. Stairfoot was an established communication centre, so there was relatively easy

access by road from the factory gate to all major routeways. The Barnsley to Barnetby railway had been completed in 1851 but with coal being a lucrative source of business for the new rail companies a complex web of industrial lines and sidings evolved running by and almost encircling the growing works. The Barnsley coal railway extension (1870), the famous 'Stairfoot Curve' (1882) and especially the Houghton Main colliery branch line (1892) — carried by an embankment over Grange Lane — are prominent landscape features.

Almost in shot, in the bottom left corner of Plate 5, overlooking the railway, is the pit bank containing the two drawing shafts of the old Oaks Colliery. The Barnsley coal seam was reached at about 290 yards in late 1841, at the expense of William Micklethwaite of Ardsley who sold out to Messers Firth, Barber and Company in 1845. The pit had an abysmal safety record, even by the standards of the of the day, culminating in the explosions of 11-12 December, 1866 when 361 men and boys were killed in what remains England's worst mining disaster. Thus when Rylands was establishing his glassworks the nearby communities of Hoyle Mill, Ardsley and Monk Bretton had been devastated by this great tragedy. The colliery company sunk a new pit (the New Oaks) off Wombwell Lane in 1870 which functioned until about 1910, the site occupied by Yorkshire Tar Distillers until that plant closed in 1970. The old Oaks site was absorbed by Rylands Main Colliery Company and then Barnsley Main.

In mid-Victorian Britain glassworkers usually worked a basic 48 or 54 hour week via two six hour shifts and for practical and technical reasons had to live near to their place of work. By the 1880s, through the Stairfoot Artisan Dwelling Company, comfortable housing had been built for Rylands' employees. Workers' cottages such as Tank Row can be seen on the aerial view, almost within the shadow of the main chimney. Shaftesbury Street and (out of shot) Gordon Street,

Above: Getting ready for the visit of King George V and Queen Mary : Rylands works in 1912.

formed part of a little community near Stairfoot [canal] Bridge known locally as 'Treacle Town' where skilled workers (regarded by some as 'stuck-up') and their families resided. Two Methodist chapels: on Barnsley Road and Hunningley Lane, stamped an unmistakeable air of nonconformity on this working class area.

Rylands' most important initial task would have been to recruit key teams of skilled men. Some would have been poached from nearby bottleworks but glassmakers were an exceptionally mobile labour force. Denis Ashurst, in his recent book *The History of South*

Yorkshire Glass cites the example of Cudworth-born Matthew Lowe who had glassmaking experience at Bristol, Castleford, Mexborough and Swinton prior to his arrival at Rylands but was only 32 years old. There was also a strong tradition of sons following fathers in the trade over several generations. Mr Arthur Boylan started work at Wood Brothers at the age of fourteen, in 1928, earning nine shillings (45p) for a 47 hour week but his father had begun work at Rylands in 1893. Child labour and apprentices were used extensively during the nineteenth century, though after 1878 children aged

Above: Arthur Boylan, young Woods Bros glassworker.

8-13 years were restricted to half-time hours and there was a maximum 12 hour day for young persons over the age of fourteen. When the Hope Works opened the average wage in the industry was 28-30 shillings (£1.40-£1.50) per week which compared very favourably with other trades: miners, 21-23 shillings (£1.05-£1.15); farm labourers, 14 shillings (60p) per week. Actual pay, however, was via a complicated piecework system.

By 1874 Rylands was manufacturing, under licence, a self-stoppering bottle invented by soda manufacturer Hiram Codd (1838-1887) of Islington. A marble, placed in the upper part of the bottle was forced up against a rubber ring in the neck under pressure of the aerated contents. The consumer was able to repeatedly reach the fizzy drink by depressing the marble via a purpose-made wooden peg (or otherwise cunning manipulation). The bottle was 'waisted' to stop the marble falling to the bottom and subsequent modifications prevented the marble rolling back into the neck while the drink was being poured. Codd and Rylands formed a partnership in 1877 and the Codd bottle became immensley popular, especially with children who also coveted, despite considerable danger, the left-over marble which could only be obtained by smashing the glass. The marbles were supplied initially from works in London and, from 1895, were specially made by Tomlinson's Manor Flint Glassworks, conveniently located at the Wombwell side of Stairfoot. Since Codds were used solely for mineral water beer drinkers began referring to weak beer as 'codswallop' and a slang word was born, though its origin in the latest edition of *The Concise Oxford Dictionary of Current English* is given as 'unknown'.

Many other firms took out licences using Codd's patent and there were numerous new patented and rogue makers. Locally, for example, versions were produced by Redfearns and the Oaks Glass Bottle Works of Hoyle Mill. Early Rylands' bottles had the number '4' on them, representing the qualities of neatness, cleanliness, accuracy and strength.

After Benjamin's death, in 1881, the business passed to his very able son, Daniel whose original ideas and business sense resulted in remarkable technological and product improvements, though not without disputes with his partner, Codd, and the Rylands' workforce. In 1885, for example, his design to feed molten glass to a semi-automatic machine (and therefore to away with the traditional 'gatherer' who traditionally got most pay for his skills) did not always work. The introduction of the tank furnace meant that molten glass was available continuosly, and bulk, round the clock production was possible. Gas replaced coal in the new furnaces enabling a more stable temperature to be maintained. Two gas-holders can be seen in the aerial view, standing slightly apart from the main buildings. The Hope Works was booming. Between 1884-1888 production more

Above: Hoyle Mill Road in Edwardian Times.

Below: Apprenticeship Indenture of William Charles Plowright and Dan Rylands, 1885. *(M. Wigglesworth)*

This Indenture made the *fifth* day of *October* 1885

BETWEEN *William Charles Plowright of Highlarque* of *Woodburn, near Barnsley*, in the County of *York* and *William Charles Plowright* her son of the one part, and DAN RYLANDS of Hope Glass Works, Stairfoot, in Ardsley, near Barnsley, in the County of York, Glass Bottle Manufacturer, of the other part

WITNESSETH that the said *William Charles Plowright* (hereinafter called "the apprentice") hath of his own free will and with the consent of the said *William Plowright* put and bound himself to and with the said DAN RYLANDS (hereinafter called "the master") for the term of *three years and seven months* to be computed from the date of these presents, during all which term the apprentice shall and will serve the master faithfully, keep his secrets, observe his lawful commands, forbear to do him hurt or injury either to his person or property, attend regularly and diligently to his affairs and interests, account honestly for all money, goods and effects which shall be committed to his charge, and deliver up the same as and when required so to do, and in every respect conduct himself as an industrious and trustworthy apprentice. AND the master in consideration of such service as aforesaid and of the covenant of the said *William Plowright* hereinafter contained, does hereby covenant with the said *William Plowright* and also with the apprentice, that he the master will teach and instruct the apprentice or cause him to be taught and instructed in the art and business of Glass Bottle Making which the master now uses and carries on. And also will during the said term pay to the apprentice the sum of Ten Shillings weekly during the time that he is wetting off and gathering; the sum of Eleven Shillings weekly during the time that he is gathering and blowing; the sum of Twelve Shillings weekly during the time that he is blowing all; and the sum of Thirteen Shillings weekly during the time that he is gathering all; the sum of Fifteen Shillings weekly during the time that he is bottle-making. PROVIDED, and it is hereby agreed that each week's work shall consist of five journeys or days or turns of not less than nine-and-a-half hours each working time; except, however, when short time is ordered or other alterations in the time are made by the master. PROVIDED ALSO, and it is hereby agreed between the parties hereto, that when the master so requires, the apprentice shall work six journeys or days or turns, of not less than nine-and-a-half hours each week, but for the work done on the sixth journey or day or turn, the apprentice shall be paid *all plus*. AND the said *William Plowright* doth hereby covenant with the master that she will during the said term, find and provide for the apprentice proper and sufficient meat, drink, lodging, and washing, and clothing and wearing apparel, suitable to his station in life, and all necessary physic, medicine, nursing and surgery.

IN WITNESS whereof the parties to these presents have hereunto set their hand and seals the day and year first above written.

SIGNED, Sealed, and Delivered by the *William Charles Plowright*
said *Wm Chas Plowright*
Wm Plowright *Ann Plowright*
Dan Rylands *Dan Rylands*
in the presence of
Ralph Rawling Blackburn

than doubled as did the size of the factory. The detached building by the gate of the factory was used for the making of wooden bottle cases (a seperate 'box factory', which, along with its chimney can be seen to the right of the main works, was later built by the Rylands Glass and Engineering Company). Rylands' workforce, however, were by no means happy with all the changes, culminating in the strike of 1886 and a court case which Rylands lost. He refused to set on union members and paid his non-union men one shilling extra per week. In 1888 the family business became a limited company with Dan Rylands as managing director.

In the 1880s a semi-automatic bottle-making machine,

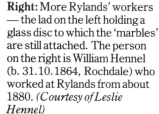

Above: Workers, some as young as fourteen, making bottles at Rylands.

Right: More Rylands' workers — the lad on the left holding a glass disc to which the 'marbles' are still attached. The person on the right is William Hennel (b. 31.10.1864, Rochdale) who worked at Rylands from about 1880. *(Courtesy of Leslie Hennel)*

Left: William Charles Plowright, former Rylands glassworker. *(M. Wigglesworth)*

invented by William Ashley, which only required two unskilled labourers to operate and could producing 200 bottles per hour (doubling production) was gaining the support of the glass companies. Rylands appreciated the need for further capital investment in new technology but understandable worker resistance combined with growing financial problems lead to his resignation at the age of 43 in 1892, followed by personal bankruptcy after which he attempted suicide at his home, Shepcote House (mid-right side of Plate 5). Described as a 'tragic genius' by Denis Ashurst in a recent study in *Aspects of Barnsley* (Wharncliffe Publishing Ltd, 1993) he continued to suffer mental illness, fatally cutting his throat with a razor, in 1910.

Frank Wood (of Wood Bros) had bought Rylands' in 1905 and by the early 1920s new concrete sheds (Number 7 shop) housed some of the latest machinery. The company's great mistake was in continuing to concentrate on production of the Codd bottle despite growing use of the crown cap, alternative stopper bottles and especially the screw top. The installation of two fully automatic Owen machines failed to live up to production expectations. By the 1920s the Codd bottle had gone out of fashion and it would take more than a symbolic wooden peg to release the once-famous works from closure.

Mr J.K. Leach who worked on the night shift at Rylands in its last two years of operation recalled some of the working conditions when interviewed by the *Barnsley Chronicle* in 1988:

'Its no joke for a young lad fresh from school having to run all night through with red-hot bottles at the end of a long fork and get them into a kiln before they cracked. A pair of boots would only last three weeks on that job.'

Below: The royal party arrives in Barnsley.

The Rylands workers were renown for singing, their voices attracting royal approval in 1912 when King George V and Queen Mary visited the works. "The Queen said she was intrigued to hear untrained voices singing so beautifully. They [the workmen] sang 'Will You No' Come Back Again' and 'Kind, Kind and Gentle is She'," said Mr Leach. The singing stopped in 1927, as when a cloth is placed over a bird in its cage, at a workplace which in its hey-day harboured more than a thousand voices.

Left: The King engaged in conversation with Alderman Raley.

Left: Montage of the royal visit composed by Barnsley photographer Warner Gothard. *(Brian Elliott Collection)*

Right: Widow of Thomas Hyde, photographed when she was about 85 years old, 60 years after the Oaks Colliery disaster of 1866. Thomas, a pit sinker, came to Hoyle Mill from Swadlincote, Derbyshire to work at the Oaks but within six months lost his life. His body was recovered eighteen months later, identified by a darned patch on his trousers. Both he and his wife were aged 25 with two young children. *(Elliott Collection)*

On 31 October 1929, seventeen days after the R101, the world's biggest airship, made her maiden voyage over London (and a week after the New York Stock Ehange crashed), a less well-known flight was made over the Barnsley side of Stairfoot. The aircrews' mission was to photograph the redundant Rylands works. In this close view (Plate 6), taken from the south, the main factory buildings appear intact and in a reasonable state of repair. A small group of young men, lead by Alec Clark, were in fact in the midst of carrying out a major refurbishment programme after the family firm of Beatson Clark of Masborough, Rotherham had obtained possession of the Rylands site ten months earlier. In a most remarkable transformation bottles were once more being produced, beginning on 26 October, 1930. Trading as Beatson Clark PLC (since 1989 part of the Tyzack Turner group), round-the-clock production of glass containers at the modern Stairfoot works, Hoyle Mill Lane continues to the present day.

Let us now go back a little: Beatson Clark had made an offer to purchase Rylands 'as a going concern' in 1927 which would have included the use of recently installed automatic machines; but, following lengthy discussions, there was no agreement. After closure everything was offered for sale barring production machinery which had been seized by the group holding the Owen rights. The Wakefield scrap dealer who bought the works removed some of the more accessible girders but instead of demolishing the factory preferred a faster return on his investment, selling the freehold of the land and the empty shells of buildings to Beatson Clark who then abandoned any plans to build a new plant by their Rotherham works.

The huge task of refitting the Stairfoot works was entrusted to Alec W Clark who recalled the dreadful state of the buildings in his book *Through a Glass Clearly* in 1980:

> 'This [the large modern concrete structure] was in a terrible state, having been totally gutted. There were great holes in the floor where the annealing furnaces had been, but we bought it in the belief that it could be converted to our use . . . Today it is difficult to picture the dismal conditions in that huge shop during the early days'

Starting a new venture during a period of worsening economic depression must have been a daunting prospect for Mr Clark who not only directed operations but worked alongside the men. Clark, however, acknowledged that there were two important local advantages: first, the Barnsley Main Colliery and its adjacent coking plant was conveniently situated only a quarter of a mile away. Rylands had been using coke oven gas for boiler firing and this vital arrangement could continue with the minimum of overheads. Secondly, there was, in his words 'a steady fund of strong young men, ready, able and willing to take on any job they could possibly perform'.

A few experienced hands were transferred from the Rotherham works but would have had to make their own way to the works prior to finding lodgings. Neil York, currently employed at Beatson Clark, told the writer how his grandfather, Maurice Hutchinson (1908-71) used to cycle every day from Whiston to

Below: Beatson Clark Glassworks c.1947: Rylands Number 7 Shop (used by Beatsons as Number 1 Shop). Alec Clark on the right. *(Neil York)*

Stairfoot along with workmate Edgar Rollinson. Maurice worked in the maintenance and sorting department. There were only a small band of young men, perhaps eight 'founder members' of the new workforce. Others included 'Bert' Day, a Rotherham 'taker-in' (who became a skilled 'teazer' or furnace-man), Milford Clark and, a local man, George Evans. Gradually, as production began, more locals were employed, mostly lads of sixteen to eighteen years old, sixteen being the minimum age allowed for shift-work. Initially the pay was three shillings (15p) per week at the age of sixteen, rising by sixpence at seventeen and, 'if they were good enough. . .otherwise someone else was set on', four shillings (20p) at the age of eighteen. Some of the new recruits, such as Roy Weston, Jack Huntington and Bill Duncan rose to become foremen or production managers.

For some young school leavers the prospect of getting a job at the new works, and perhaps an apprenticeship, must have had a great appeal. But with demand far eeeding supply the firm could afford to be selective, and had no need to advertise: 'word of mouth' was a most effective way of directing any new openings to potential employees. Personal ingenuity also played a great part in getting a job — in itself regarded a good test of a lad's determination and interest. The case of young Benjamin Kitching, keen as mustard to get a job at Beatsons, serves as a good example. Ben's newspaper round included a delivery to Beatson nightwatchman Herbert Myers, an old Rylands worker whom Ben thought was nightshift manager. The schoolboy kept asking Mr Myers to 'remember me if there are any jobs going'. Another Beatson worker, Bill Parks, who later became yard foreman, came to live near Ben, in Field Lane. Bill began organising amateur dramatics in Ardsley church hall which attracted Ben's interest and was therefore asked to 'put a good word in' on his behalf.

Benjamin Kitching left Mark Street school shortly

Above: Ben Kitching, b.1917

after his fourteenth birthday, in September, 1931 but found himself helping his father filling sacks of coal in Barnsley Goods Station, a 'job' that he was far from pleased about. Then, on Thursday 1st October, a letter was delivered to Ben's house asking him to report to Beatsons the same afternoon. After a quick 'swill in a bucket' but still wearing overalls and short trousers, Ben walked the short distance to the factory. His interview with works manager Alec Clark, a Congregationalist, was brief and to the point:

Clark: "Are you working?"

Ben : "No. I'm only helping my father with coal".

Clark: "If you were working we can not give you a job. Which church do you attend?"

Ben : "I go to Ardsley church"

The aspiring engineer showed Mr Clark his school report which suggested that metalwork was his best subject. He was told to start work on Monday morning, 5 October, 1931 and would receive nine shillings (45p) for a 54 hour working week.

Ben Kitching spent a good deal of his time under the direction of 'foreman fitter' Harold Cocker, a highly respected engineer who eventually became works manager; but Ben's work as a fourteen year old was far from routine: 'One minute I was fitting pipes and the next sent up on the roof to patch-up a hole because it was raining in; then off to unload great 2½ cwt sacks of soda ash from railway wagons, wheeling them away and stacking them up'. Eventually he completed a seven year apprenticeship, qualifying as a skilled mould-maker, responsible for the mould shop, retiring in 1982 after

51 years of almost continuous employment. He is probably the last surviving member of the early Beatson Clark workforce at Stairfoot.

After experimenting with automatic Monish machines at the Rotherham works two Monish Majors were installed at Stairfoot. On this machine, a team of one man and two boys (an operator, a taker-out and taker-in) could produce 4,000 standard medicine bottles in an eight hour shift, a significant improvement over mouth-blown manufacture which required a large team or chair of men. Ben Kitching recalled that 'an expert' would occasionally arrive from Scotland to sort out teething problems but it was the young fitters who really kept production going. These were the first machines that could put a neck on a bottle, a job that previously had to be done by hand. A piece inserted in the mould enabled the name of chemists to be embossed on one side of the bottle but a careful watch had to be made to ensure that the production run, allowing for rejects, was not eeeded. Alec Clark recalled that early

Below: Maurice Hutchinson inspecting bottles. *(Neil York)*

production was inefficient, particularly because 'our sorting standards were based on mouth blown practice'. Enormous mountains of cullet (broken, reject glass) was a 'depressing and visible daily reminder of how badly we were doing'.

A great deal of engineering ingenuity enabled five ounce bottles, to the requirements of the Bronnley company, to be made on the Monish machine, although the efficiency of production, according to Clark, 'was extremely low'. Yet, late in 1931, following the ending of important duties, William Maier, the German director of the International Bottle Company Limited of London was so impressed with the production of the Bronnley bottle at Stairfoot that Beatson Clark were regarded as the ideal home supplier for his company.

In 1932, following the retirement of his father, Alec Clark was appointed a director but became increasingly concerned with 'the cash flow situation' at Stairfoot. Fred Sweeting, office manager during the period when Clark was works manager, had developed a semi-automatic machine known as Sweeting-Hardman in his previous employment at Castleford. This machine was installed close to the two Monish Majors. A hand gatherer was able to gather glass from the furnace and drop it in the Sweeting machine where, in the words of Alec Clark 'a second skilled man could snip it off and

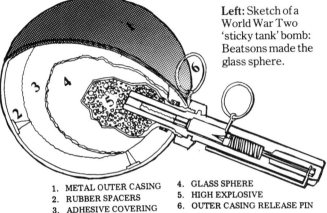

Left: Sketch of a World War Two 'sticky tank' bomb: Beatsons made the glass sphere.

1. METAL OUTER CASING
2. RUBBER SPACERS
3. ADHESIVE COVERING
4. GLASS SPHERE
5. HIGH EXPLOSIVE
6. OUTER CASING RELEASE PIN

form the parison [bubble of molten glass] before transferring it into the blowing mould where a boy would blow it into shape'. This process, for a few special products, extended production capacity at a crucial time. Workers, most of them known personally by Sweeting were employed from the Castleford area for this process. Semi-automatic machines were also occasionally used, for making glass stoppers which were placed in chemists' shop rounds and storage jars. The stoppers were ground individually at Rotherham, after skilled mouldmaking and pressing at Stairfoot. During the war semi-automatic machines were turned over to making glass 'sticky' or incendiary bombs which were filled with sulphur; and the fitting shop was converted to make parts for aircraft tanks.

Beatson Clark owes a great deal to the ingenuity of its small pioneer workforce under the leadership of Alec Clark during the formative years of its existence at Stairfoot. Dan Rylands would have been proud of their considerable achievements.

Below: 'Stairfoot, 1944' by Henry Rushburg R.A. A painting of women in wartime at the Stairfoot works, depicting Monish machines in operation.

Above: I.S. (Individual Section) machines at work at Stairfoot, about 1947.

This low-level oblique view was taken on Wednesday 25 May 1938, three weeks after parliament approved the Anglo-Italian Agreement, attacked by Labour as 'A sell-out to Fascism'; and four months before Chamberlain promised 'Peace for our time'.

Few towns have such a conspicious public building as Barnsley Town Hall which was constructed during 1932-33. It was built alongside the new Mining and Technical College (1930-32), both structures to the design of the same Liverpool man. The transformation of the whole west side of Church Street, which began with widening and slum clearances a decade earlier was now complete. The use by architects Briggs and Thornley of large blocks of [oolitic] limestone as facing material was a deliberate ploy to give the town hall a distinctive appearance amid the darkened brick and sandstone of old buildings. Portland stone, the most famous of English building material (used by Wren on St Paul's), achieves its most striking effect through contrast. It becomes whiter when washed by rain, though atmospheric pollution was already having an effect on the appearance of the great twenty-one bay front and landmark tower.

The Neo-Classical design may not have appealed to the taste of architectural historian Professor Pevsner, especially the tower of diminishing stages 'carried uneasily on a facade which in its stylistic character cannot have anything to do with towers'. An architect's drawing in Barnsley Archives suggests that a more ornate tower had been offered, resembling the towers of the Royal Liver Building in Liverpool where Briggs & Thornley had their offices. The tower had in fact been omitted from the design on the grounds of economy and did not receive council approval until July 1932, four months after the foundation stone ceremony. In any event the clock tower emphasises the commanding site of the building — and is perhaps more in keeping with the Barnsley character.

The cost of building and furnishing the town hall was £188,000, a huge sum to find during the depression when a terraced house could be built for less than £400. Yet the building was long overdue, having been discussed in council for about forty years! The old town hall, in St Mary's Gate, was described in the *Barnsley Chronicle* as 'of dingy appearance' and 'out of keeping with a County Borough of Barnsley's size and importance'. The increasing workload of the local authority had been compounded by the addition of the urban districts of Ardsley, Monk Bretton and part of Worsbrough in 1921, the Corporation's business having to be shared between several scattered buildings in the borough. In 1897 the Mayor, Charles Wray, announced that the 'The Corporation has made up its mind to proceed with the erection of the proposed Town Hall and Municipal Offices in Kendray Street and Eldon Street at the earliest possible date'. Robinsons, owners of the timber yard, were given notice to vacate their prime business site (subsequently used for the market extension) but opposition was so great that 'Wray's Scheme' was abandoned.

Below: This picture postcard of Barnsley's new Town Hall is post-marked 16 August, 1937. *(Elliott Collection)*

Town Hall, Barnsley.

In 1913, when the town achieved Borough status, the council decided to place its future civic centre in Church Street and also proposed to create a purpose-built technical college on the site of the old Manor House; but in 1916 the project was suspended pending post-war events. Building was postponed 'for an indefinite period' in 1927 because of the capital involved but representations were made for assistance from the government's Unemployment Grants Committee. By Christmas 1929 the plan for the erection of the college 'was now in hand', a contract for £79,660 having been agreed (£15,000 coming from the Miners' Welfare Fund) and in February 1930 the Ministry of Health approved

the proposals for building the new town hall, sanctioning a loan in excess of £100,000 repayable over fifty years. The council argued that building would 'assist the government in relief of the unemployment problem in the Borough', estimating that 100 men would be employed during each week of construction. Young men such as Ernest Gill and Eric Watling (both aged 26) were glad to find work as joiners rather than face life on the dole.

The town hall foundation stone was laid on Thursday 21 April 1932. A special stand was erected with seating for several hundred guests along with a raised platform, draped in colours of red, white and blue, to accommodate

the 'principals' taking part in the ceremony. The stone was laid by the Mayor of Barnsley, Councillor Robert Jonas Plummer, J.P. using the same level and mallet handled by the late King Edward VII at Liverpool Cathedral thirty years earlier. In his speech Mayor Plummer congratulated the architects 'of this noble and inspiring building', suggesting that when present and future councillors 'are deliberating upon its (the borough's) affairs may they also be inspired by noble thoughts and deeds'.

In its report of the occasion, illustrated by architects drawings, the *Barnsley Chronicle* provided readers with an insight of the internal arrangement of the new seat of local government. The central entrance would lead to 'a spacious entrance hall and staircase'. Most of the ground floor was to be occupied by the Borough Collector's and Accountant's departments, the rest to Education, Health and Weights & Measures. The Council Chamber was placed in a central position on the first floor but at the rear of the building 'in order to obtain the necessary quietude'. Five committee rooms, the Mayor's Parlour and a central reception room occupied 'practically the entire length of the Church Street facade', the remaining space used by the Town Clerk's and Borough Surveyor's departments. The second floor housed the kitchen, Water Engineer's suite, caretaker's flat and spare offices. For safety and comfort the building was to have 'fire-proof floors, heated by low pressure hot water pipes, supplied by radiators'.

The Mining and Technical College opened on Monday 10 October 1932. The official opening ceremony, which took place two years and two months after the laying of the foundation stone, was performed by Sir Michael Sadler and Mayor Robert Plummer. Alderman Herbert Smith and Henry Walker, architect Mr H Thornley, College Principal D P Grubb and Director of Education Evan Davies were among the platform party. 'This

Below: The Town Hall foundation stone ceremony: 21 April, 1932: Mayor Robert Plummer, Town Clerk Albert D. Mason.

Above: An early view of Church Street before re-development, c. 1910. *(Elliott Collection)*

College', said Sir Michael, 'will rank alongside the best schools of learning in the country [and] will stir the imagination and awaken the mental facilities. . .of thousands of young men and young women, and beget within them healthy ambitions, lofty ideals, and noble aspirations'. In the Special Supplement produced by the *Barnsley Chronicle* the builder, Charles Smith, who employed local labour, was praised for his achievement.

The 'largest Mining College in the country' would serve 'some hundred square miles of South Yorkshire'. Apart from mining there were departments of electrical engineering, building, chemistry and physics, commerce and domestic science, geered to meet increasing vocational needs. 'Belle Vue', a stone mansion at the top of Cockerham Lane was purchased and adapted for the teaching of housecraft. Before 1932 'The Technical

Right: 'Technical College, Barnsley', from a 1930s postcard. *(Elliott Collection)*

Left: This photograph was probably taken on the same day as the foundation laying ceremony. *(Eric Gill)*

Right: The tower, covered with scaffolding, nears completion. *(Eric Gill)*

Below: Site joiners. *(Elliott Collection*

Far Right: Site carpenter Eric Gill used his imagination when taking this unusual view through the opening made for the Town Hall clock.

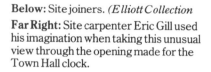

School' as it was then known, was housed in the Harvey Institute (Public Hall, Eldon Street) and in a variety of scattered temporary premises. Built predominantly of brick, the 'old college' remains an imposing architectural feature, despite the shadow of the town hall.

The Town Hall opened on Thursday 14 December 1933: 'Yesterday will ever linger in the minds of Barnsley people. It will remain an inspiring memory, marked as it was by a unity of purpose and a common impulse on the part of the citizens. The day was of eagerly anticipated visit of His Royal Highness the Prince of Wales, and during a two hour stay in the town the Prince, with a golden key, unlocked the door of Barnsley's new Town Hall, this inaugurating what is expected to be a new civic era' *(Barnsley Chronicle)*.

Flags were said to have 'floated from the summit of all the main buildings of the town' and many shops and houses put on decorative displays. A large hoarding at the top of Regent Street, provided by the Chronicle, had the greeting 'WELCOME TO HRH PRINCE OF WALES'. The Prince 'looking very fit' wore 'dark blue Ulster with astrakham collar, tweed suit, suede shoes, green check muffler and a bowler hat, and many times. . .a radiant smile lit up his tanned features'.

The Prince of Wales arrived in Barnsley (from Harewood House) about noon, meeting councillors, members of the Council of Social Services and Trades and Labour Council and visited the new Nelson Street premises of the Barnsley Boys' Club. His lunch menu, devised by Mr & Mrs J L Thornhill of the Royal Hotel consisted of a Barnsley chop, chips, tea and toast followed by peach melba and cheese and biscuits. Mrs Janet Warburton, Head Cook at the Royal, prepared the meal whilst head waitress Ethel Monks, aged nineteen waited on the Prince at table. Afterwards the Prince's health was toasted by Councillor Herbert Smith and Councillor Plummer presented him with a miniature miner's electric lamp in sterling silver. Responding, the

Below: The Prince of Wales, Mayor John Guest and guests pose for photographs on the Town Hall steps: 14 December, 1933.

Above: The top of Regent Street at the junction with Church Street, c. 1916, before later demolition and re-development. *(Elliott Collection)*

Below: The new Barnsley Permanent Building Society headquarters, completed in 1936. *(BMBC)*

Above: Albert Hirst (left) and his brother prepare the 'royal' Barnsley chops. *(BMBC)*

Prince jokingly said that he was 'somewhat alarmed' when faced with the prospect of consuming a Barnsley chop and sought assurances from the mayor (John Guest) that no fine would ensue 'for not finishing it'. When the Prince arrived at the Town Hall at about 1.30 pm the entire length of Market Hill was 'filled with an eager and enthusiastic crowd' whilst children were 'accommodated in front of barriers, in the care of friendly policemen, and sellers of miniature Union Jacks and replicas of the Prince's feathers did a brisk trade'. After the unlocking ceremony the royal guest was presented with a gold key, on behalf of the Corporation, by Councillor Joseph Jones, CBE, JP. For many people the visit resulted in happy memories at a time when unemployment and poverty was common. Writing to the *Barnsley Chronicle* from his Sussex home in 1987, Mr Raymond Jackson (b. 1921) who attended Racecommon Road Council School recalled being given a guided tour of the new building along with his school chums, coming away with a bar of chocolate and a commemorative medal. His first job, aged fourteen, was at the Globe Tea Co. in May Day Green for 7s. 6d. (37½p) per week, significantly advanced to £1 in 1937 when he secured an employment at Wood Bros Glass Works.

Two other 'white' 1930s buildings catch the eye. The

headquarters of the Barnsley Permanent Building Society (now Barnsley Building Society), completed 1935-36 to J R Wilkinson's design, dominate the corner of Church Street and Regent Street on a prime site which had been available for development since 1924 when 'Dr Sadler's' house was pulled down. The Exchange Building (D L Evans Drapers, now Halifax Building Society), at the junction of Market Hill and Shambles Street, stands out in the aerial view, though its upper facade is rarely noticed at street level. It replaced the Corn Exchange which, as we have seen, was destroyed by fire in December, 1927.

We are also given a fine view of the large area of open space known as Fair Field, used for trade and recreational purposes since medieval times. It formed the south part of the great Church Field. Fair Field was the traditional site of the September Michaelmas fair, said to be noted for the sale of horses, sheep and cattle as well as a variety of fresh and dry produce including onions, herbs and pears, all brought in by cart, packhorse and yoke. The marking of St Michael the Archangel's Day by eating a goose dinner was adopted by Barnsley people, the district becoming noted for 'goose pyes'. By mid-Victorian times some activities in 'Church Field', such as football, knur and spell and tip cat (a game in which a short sharp-ended piece of wood, the 'cat', is tipped in the air with a stick) were causing alarm to residents and bypassers. A complaint of 'improper conduct' was made to the Board of Health in July 1859 because (the previous day) 'a large number of people were there congregated engaged in games nearly all nude, and cursing and swearing'.

Above Left: Regent Street from the Town Hall tower. *(Eric Gill)*

Above: The King and Queen leave the Mining and Technical College in October 1937. Mr Joseph Jones, Mayor and Mr Adam Eric Gilfillan the new Town Clerk wait by the car. *(Elliott Collection)*

Right: The Bus Station before and after completion. *(Yorkshire Traction)*

Before swooping low towards Church Street the aircraft was at a convenient height for its cameraman to take a spectacular view of the changing town (Plate Eight). The new town hall and college are dominating features. St Mary's church is almost lost amid a boundary of trees. Market stalls and shoppers can be seen on Market Hill, May Day Green, the Gas Nook and on both sides of Kendray Street (fish and fruit markets), Wednesday being market day. We have a fine view of the compact complex of old buildings between the west side of the market place and Graham's Orchard.

The lower half of the aerial photograph makes interesting comparison with Plate One, taken ten years earlier. A most important development is apparent between Queens Road and Exchange Station, and east of the railway viaduct — work was in progress on Barnsley's new omnibus station. The contractors, William Johnson and Son of Park Street Works, Wombwell, had excavated 11,000 tons of material within five weeks of starting the project on 27 October 1937. The town badly needed a 'bus station; starting stands for expanding services had to operate from Church Street, Peel Street, Doncaster Road, Midland Street, Eldon Street, Kendray Street and the Gas Nook, competing with an increasing number of private cars and goods vehicles.

At the time the Bus Station opened, on Wednesday 13 December 1938, it was considered to be the best in Yorkshire and undoubtedly added to the amenities of the town. 'Special attention' was made by the company to provide adequate toilet facilities 'with hot water available in the ladies room'. Godley's took charge of the catering facilities, described as 'one of the greatest assets' of the station. Their cafe had a seating area for one hundred, 'supplying anything in the way of food from a sandwich to a hot luncheon'. Haigh Bros operated two newspaper kiosks in the new bus station, the one

AEROFILMS

Right: Driver and conductress 'pass time' by the Ward Green service bus, Eldon Street c. 1935. *(Yorkshire Traction)*

Above: 1935 Leyland T57 with C. H. Roe Ltd body, 32 seats. *(Yorkshire Traction)*

on the centre island was known locally as the 'threepenny bit' and served as a rendesvous point for courting couples. Another retail feature in the environs of the new bus station was the fruiterers known as 'Mrs Platts'. Barnsley, according to its local newspaper, 'will become a hub of a far reaching travel system carrying millions of people a year'. Four platforms (A, B, C and D) were linked by 'safety crossings . . . so that pedestrians will stand no risk of being jammed or knocked down'. The Yorkshire Traction Company, under the leadership of General Manager Mr G W Robinson (appointed in 1928) was justly proud of its achievement. It was anticipated that the maximum arrival and departure of vehicles would be around 3,000 per day, but it was soon to become very congested.

Below: Peel Square from Chronicle buildings, 1930s. *(Elliott Collection)*

Above: Yorkshire Traction 'double-decker', 1930. *(Yorks Traction)*

Below: Three Cranes Hotel, Royal Oak and F. W. Woolworth & Co Ltd, Queen Street. *(Tasker Collection)*

During the 1930s the fleet strength increased from 200 to almost 300 vehicles and after 1935 unit costs were reduced with the introduction of diesel-engined buses.

It was during the thirties that a number of notable chain stores were established in Barnsley and as a consequence some of the smaller shops began to disappear. In 1930 the corner of Eldon Street and Queen Street was transformed when the distinctive Montague Burton building (now McDonalds) was erected, the gleaming white 'livery' of the upper floors clearly visible from the air. About the same time F W Woolworth & Company Limited built their original Barnsley store on the site of the Royal Oak Yard, near the Eldon Street entrance of Burlington Arcade. 'Woolies', the Royal Oak and Three Cranes Hotel, extended through to Queen Street, their contrasting facades evident in our aerial view. Opposite side of the road from Burtons can be seen the white stone upper edging of Marks & Spencer's frontage, established in 1937. It was built on the site of the White Swan Inn and two small shops. The rooftop and part of the south side of the other Burton store (which became Jackson The Tailors) on Cheapside, facing May Day Green, can also be seen sandwiched between smaller and long established retailers. Cheapside received a further new look in 1939 when Littlewoods opened their modern white fronted store, which resulted in the demolition of several elderly properties shown in the aerial view.

At the Eldon street end of the fish market a large new stone building can be seen, This was occupied from 1936 to 1939 by furnishers H Lewis & Son, later known as Willsons Fashion House. It was cleared as part of the development of the Metropolitan Centre in 1973-74, Superdrug currently trading from the site.

The re-vamped Wire Trellis Hotel, resplendent in white facing material, is easily identifiable at the bottom right of the picture, the work completed during publican Fred Moxon's tenancy.

Far Right: Queen's Street. *(Elliott Collection)*
Right: The 'new' Wire Trellis Hotel. *(Tasker Collection)*

This view (Plate Nine) was taken on Sunday 24 October 1937, at a time when the Duke of Windsor (who, as the Prince of Wales, had opened Barnsley Town Hall) and his wife, the former Mrs Wallace Simpson were being entertained in Nazi Germany and had had a cordial meeting with the

Below: The spectacular neon facade of the Ritz in 1937. *(A. Steele)*

Fuehrer. In Barnsley about half the population were escaping from the drudgery of everyday life by going to the cinema at least once a week. The great new attraction, opposite Taylor's mill on Peel Street, had a long entrance leading to an auditorium and stage contained in a large building with 'RITZ' emblazoned on the slope of its roof — even passing aircraft couldn't miss it!

With its neon-lit Art Deco front, glorious foyer and plush interior the new "Ritz" was an outstanding specimen of cinema architecture. It was designed by Messers F Verity and S Beverley to the requirements of Mr J H Lundy, Director of Theatre Construction to Union Cinemas Ltd., in consultation with H F Tulley, the company's staff architect. On its grand opening, Monday 22 March 1937, patrons entered the building 'through a double line of glass doors. . . into the spacious main vestibule, which leads to the stalls on the ground floor, and to the grand staircases to the balcony'. The 'wealth and warmth' apparent in the foyers was repeated in the auditorium where the luxurious decor was 'enhanced by the artistic use of mirrors and a most attractive lighting scheme'. An intimate effect was achieved through subtle use of colour: 'graded tones of terra cotta, peach and gold, with seats and carpets in harmony'. The main feature 'reproduced on the new wonder Western Electric MIRROPHONIC sound system' was the comedy hit *My Man Godfrey* which starring William Powell, with special gala seats from one shilling (5p).

Going to the 2,000 seater super-cinema was an experience enhanced by the magical appearance of the Wurlitzer organ. Ritz projectionist Ernest Barker, formerly of Sheffield Road but now living in Southend-on-Sea, started his showbiz life at the age of fourteen as a uniformed 'pageboy' at the Alhambra Cinema (see Plate Ten). He recalled, in Kath Parkin's 'All Our Yesterdays' feature in the *Barnsley Chronicle*

Below: Ernest Barker 'plays' the Ritz Wurlitzer. *(E. Barker)*

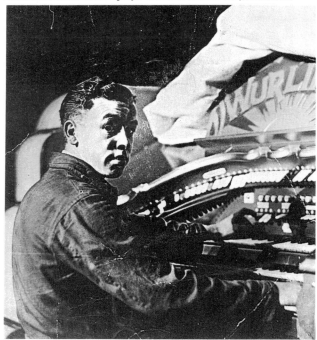

(21.5.93) how thrilled he was to 'bring up the Wurlitzer' for a press photo session in 1937: 'What a wonderful feeling it was to be seated at this organ in the glare of the spotlights' — even though he couldn't play a note! Celebrity organist H. Robinson Cleaver was engaged for its opening night, Monday 26 April 1937 and as the console came into view on its lift, with the illuminated sides glowing with changing colours, the audience broke into spontaneous applause, Robbie playing his signature tune, *An Earful of Music*.

The first resident organist was Norman Townsend, followed by Arthur Manning and, for a short period, Jack Fretwell. However, the man most associated with the Ritz Wurlitzer was ex-Elsecar miner Trevor Willetts who in 1943 was engaged on a part-time basis but four

years later appointed full-time Musical Director. He remained resident until 1962, making several broadcasts for the B.B.C. Trevor's signature tune was *We'll All Go Riding on a Rainbow.* The Wurlitzer was removed in 1969 and is now in private hands.

Another Ritz 'veteran', Alf Steele, was employed as its first pageboy working six days a week for 12s.6d. (62½p), responsible to the manager, Douglas Revie. Alfred, in a feature article written by *Chronicle* reporter Bill Blow (5.6.87) 'remembered seeing to the needs' of casts of variety artistes worthy of inclusion in the Hall of Fame of the British Music Hall: George Formby, Sandy Powell, Freddie Frinton, Charlie Kunz, Old Mother Riley, Stainless Stephen and sand dancers Wilson, Keppel and Betty. Within weeks of opening the Ritz offered for the 'FIRST TIME IN BARNSLEY' a combination of live variety and screen entertainment. The big feature film was followed by the Gaumont British News and then a 'B' movie. The Wurlitzer was played during the interval, followed by a variety show — more than three hours continuous entertainment for 6d, 9d, or 1s, (2½, 3¾ or 5p) in the stalls, and 1s 3d or 1s 6d, (6½ or 7½p) in the balcony. Staff members whom Mr Steele remembered included Ann Baker, Tom Copping, Grace Gadins, Margaret Ryan, Alf Smith and Ruth Taylor.

Union Cinemas were described in the pre-opening hype as 'the most amazing company in the entertainment industry'. They were, under the leadership of managing director Fred Bernard, working overtime to establish an extensive theatre chain. On the same day that the Ritz opened the company opened a sister cinema in Chatham, having opened theatres in Belfast, Ipswich, Scunthorpe, and Brighouse 'in the last few days' with over thirty additional super cinemas forthcoming. Despite the haste each building appears to have had the same high standard of design and equipment. By 1939 there were 5,000 cinemas in Britain, some having over

Above: The plush foyer of the Ritz will evoke many readers' memories. *(Peter Ashman)*

Above: Projectors at the ready : Projection Room, Ritz Cinema, 1937. *(E. Barker)*

Right: Projection Room switchboard for House and Stage lighting. *(E. Barker)*

Above: Celebrity organist 'Robby' Cleaver. *(E. Barker)*

Above: Pageboy Alf Steele in glamorous company: Grace Gadins (left) and girl on right married Jack Copping. *(A. Steele)*

4,000 seats. Barnsley had one of the finest examples.

My earliest memories of the Ritz are of attending the Saturday morning children's club during the mid 1950s, assembling with pals in the yard enclosed by Pitt Street. Much earlier the Saturday Morning Club's recruitment song was rendered to the tune of 'Blaze Away':

Come along and join our party,

Let's enrol you as a chum.

With all your pals so gay and harty

We can hardly wait

For Saturday to come.

What fun we have at every meeting:

The good old Ritz will take some beating.

Thats why I shout:

"Whooppee!"

I'm glad that I'm a Union chum.

The Ritz closed its doors on 16 March 1974 when part of the ABC cinema chain, and like many Barnsley buildings which have generated our affection over the years was demolished, replaced by the most uninspiring of seventies supermarket 'architecture'. When all the shoppers have gone and the traffic has fled from the street feint echoes of a distant organ and cheering children may be heard in the depths of the Pioneer (CRS) Store — Peel Street will never be the same again.

Mr Arthur W. Seddon, the Ritz's last manager (c. 1960-74) died in Barnsley aged seventy-one, in November 1993.

Above: The Ritz staff assemble for their 'team' photograph at the 1937 opening — pageboy Steele in pride of place. Others include, left to right, 2nd row: Ruth Taylor (3rd), Margaret Ryan (8th), Joyce Golding (9th) and Ann Barker (14th); men, left to right — Jack Copping (6th), Len Bradley (7th), Alf Smith (11th).

Left: The Saturday morning children club members, called Barnsley Chums, seen here with (on the left) Mr Jack Field, 'Yo-Yo' Champion of Europe who visited the Ritz in 1937. *(John Threlkeld)*

Above: Robert Donat, Ralph Richardson in *The Citadel*, directed by King Vidor, was being shown on the week the Aerofilms camera aeroplane flew over.

Below: The first Ritz advertisement to appear in the *Barnsley Chronicle*, 1937.

Above: Carole Lombard, William Powell in *My Man Godfrey* directed by Gregory La Cava, was one of the films showing at the Ritz at the time the aerial photograph was taken.
Below: Popular Ritz organist Trevor Willets who played at the Ritz from 1943 to 1962. His signature tune was *We'll All Go Riding on a Rainbow*. *(Peter Ashman)*

Above: The Art Deco front of the Ritz graced Peel Street until the mid 1970s. *(Tasker Collection)*

On Friday 2 June 1939, the day before young Barnsley men had to register for possible military service, a civilian aircraft approached the town the south, drawn along by the arteries of Sheffield and Doncaster Roads. The eye of its aerial cameraman was caught by a distinctive area of suburban development. The result is a snapshot of 'working class' Barnsley, a community, or — more precisely — a series of inter-linked streets and neighbourhoods which had become largely self-contained.

Family-owned shops and small businesses offered a variety of products and services; and amenities were close at hand: religious buildings, schools, public houses and even a small cinema. Mines, glassworks, factories and other workplaces were a walk, bike or short bus journey away. Access into town was also easy when, for example, it was market day or when entertainment beckoned at grand 'picture theatres' such as The Globe and Alhambra.

Remains of the oldest housing area can be seen in the lower North-West quarter of the photograph, mainly to the West and South of the central premises of the Barnsley British Co-operative Society and the junction of Wellington Street and New Street. Here patches of open land, used as play areas by children, are a consequence of the slum clearances of a decade earlier. By late-Victorian times the 'Barebones' area between Heelis Street and Foundry Street consisted of 'unplanned', and therefore cramped housing. Whole or parts of lost streets are evident — like fossilised remains

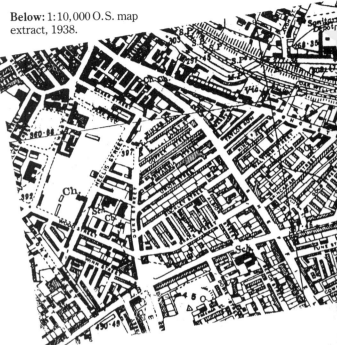

Below: 1:10,000 O.S. map extract, 1938.

Left: Sheffield Road, with fountain and horse trough at the fork with Doncaster Road. Note the arched stonework on the Alambra building and compare with the picture on page 74. *(Barnsley Archive Service)*

of a deserted medieval village: Pall Mall, Court No. 5, Oxford Square, Court No. 7 (between New Street and Silver Street); Baker Street, Raywood Row, Park Row, Lister Square, John Street, Burleigh Street, Wilson Street and Joseph Street (between Heelis and New Street).

One enterprising former resident of Heelis Street was lay-preacher Samuel Sidney Spooner who lived at house number sixteen. In the 1890s Samuel sold boiled sweets from a market stall on May Day Green, and like most traders operated from early morning until about 10 p.m. in the summer. He relied on a wheelbarrow to trundle his wares over 'cobbled' streets from home to

Sheffield Road. Barnsley. 1079.

Above:
Samuel
Sidney
Spooner,
market
trader.

market. Samuel, whose specialities included humbugs, 'big fishes' and sugar sticks also opened a small shop in Jumble Lane.

The orderly rows of houses stretching on either side of Sheffield Road were established from the late nineteenth century, bordered by 'better' properties on Park Road. Most dwellings were of course rented and, when batches occasionally came on the market, auction sale notices.

Nearer to town, some older properties can just be seen. Taylor Row, an interesting street of former weavers' cottages is evident, between Sheffield and Doncaster Roads, opposite Union Street. Rodney Row, just in view, on Doncaster Road, opposite King Street, also represents an earlier phase of housing.

Within the older housing areas, and away from Sheffield Road, the corner and mid-terrace shop was the main retail outlet. It provided goods in small quantities and anticipated that customers would be able to clear their debts on pay-day. By the late 1920s even some 'side' streets had a small shop. Alfred Winnard, for example, was a beer retailer in John Street and Joseph Priestley had a small general shop in Thomas Street whilst Harry Beaumont and Henry Walker were 'open all hours' on neighbouring Joseph Street. The main streets had several general and one or more specialised shops. Shopkeepers on Heelis Street included Abraham Bolton (No. 11), beer retailer Frank Sergeant (No. 19), Frank Fulham (No. 26), Herbert Gelder (No. 90) and grocer Martha Whittaker (No. 103). Duke Street had grocers at numbers six (Annie Addy) and nine (Walter Ogley); there was also a general shop at number twenty-two (William Harrison) whilst butcher Charles McNichol occupied number twenty-seven. On Union Street there was a confectioner (Ada Butler), a fruiterer (Isaac Darn) and a general shop (William Pyne). The passage below describes the trade of a corner shop in Salford during the early years of

Above: W. E. Horsfield 'Pawnbroker and Outfitter', 59-63 Sheffield Road: Store closed in 1971. *(Tasker Collection)*

this century but could apply to similar areas of low-income housing in Barnsley:

The very poor never fell into debt: nobody allowed them any credit. Paying on the nail, they bought in minimum quantities, sending their children usually for half a loaf, a ha'p'orth of tea, sugar, milk or a scrap of mustard pickled cauliflower in the bottom of a jar. Generally two ounces of meat or cheese was the smallest quantity one could buy; to sell less, shopkeepers said, was to lose what tiny profit they got from 'waste in cutting'. My father would not deign to attend any of these 'shipping orders', as he called them [a penn'orth of cheese for this two ounces of bacon etc]; an elder sister took indigent pence. 'It's all cash', she said briskly. Nor would Lipton or 'Sir Thomas', as my mother named him, have truck with any who tried to buy a single boot-lace or asked him to divorce a pair of kippers. Such things, he seemed to believe, came to man in natural pairs, binary as bosoms.

Robert Roberts, *The Classic Slum,* **1971.**

By the 1930s ribbon development along Sheffield Road resulted in a distinctive zone of shops and services extending towards the Park Road/Cemetery Road crossroads and beyond whereas Doncaster Road and Pontefract Road were far less commercially advanced. The following analysis, taken from Tasker's *Barnsley Streets* shows the great range of shops and services available in Sheffield Road towards the end of the decade:

Shop	Number	Shop	Number
Butchers	11	Cleaners	2
House Furnishers	9	Sweetshops	2
Confectioners	7	Greengrocer	2
Hairdressers	7	Bakers	2
Tobacconists	6	Wool	1
Outfitters	6	Milleners	1
Drapers	5	Wallpapers	1
Footwear	5	Milk Bars	1
Fruiterer	4	Wardrobe Dealers	1
Cycle/Motor Cycle	4	Photographers	1
Fish & Chips	3	Hardware	1
Newsagents	3	Chemists	1
Footwear Repair	2	Carpets	1
Libraries	2	Saddlers	1
Music	2	Watchmakers	1
Dairies	2	Toyshops	1
Fishmongers	2	Sewing Machines	1
Corn Dealers	2		

The Barnsley British Co-operative Society had its Grocery Department, Funeral and Insurance Services located in Sheffield Road. There were also two notable pawnbrokers: Horsfields and Harrals. Public houses included the Alhambra Hotel, Wharncliffe Hotel,

Above: The building on the corner is the Rising Sun Inn opened in 1862 and enlarged in 1898 when the next door was incorporated into the inn. Martha Kenworthy was the publican, 1911-46.

Clarence Hotel, Griffin Inn, Rising Sun Inn, Blackmoor Head Hotel, Old Warrior Inn, Spotted Leopard, Coach and Horses and Victoria Hotel. Charles Edward Moore, aged fifty, licensee of the Blackmoor in 1939, kept himself fit in a home-made boxing ring in an outbuilding at the back of the pub. A *Chronicle* reporter watched Charles box a couple of rounds with 'Kid' Cunningham, former light-weight champion of Scotland.

The parishes of St John (1844) and St Peter (1892) (whose brick-built church on Doncaster Road is not quite in view) were specially created to cater for the needs of this area of Barnsley. St John's church and its main school can be seen near to the junction of Joseph Street and Duke Street. Built at a cost of £3,500, St John's was consecrated in 1858. Mrs J Whewall recalled her schooldays at the church school during the 1930s in a contribution to the *Barnsley Chronicle* 'Childhood Memories' series (8.10.93):

'I remember using slate and chalk…That meant we also had felt rubbers to clean the slates…once a week. Our teacher, Mrs Ramsden, used to take us outside and we all had to bang our rubbers on the wall to get the chalk dust out of them. I also remember being able to buy a cup of Oxo instead of milk. The school also sold Gibb's toothpaste in round blocks…I was nine at the time of the coronation of King George VI in May, 1937 when each child was given a tin of toffees, a medal and a souvenir programme…we were allowed home on Coronation Day after lunch. The teachers told us that we had to offer our parents the first dip in the tin of toffees but most were opened by children on their way home. Another happy time was Christmas when, on the last day, we had Christmas pudding at our desks…'.

Understandably, chapels, some having schools, were also prominent, with examples in Heelis Street, Buckley Street and three sites on Sheffield Road, including the

Left: Typical of some of the slum dwellings that existed in Barnsley in the 1930s; this is Court 1, Baker Street. *(Barnsley Archive Service)*

Above: Ray Milland.

Above: John Howard and Heather Angel.

distinctive Ebenezer Methodist at the junction with Doncaster Road.

The highspot of the week for many local youngsters was Saturday afternoons when 'gangs' used to go to the matinee at the Star cinema, also known, colloquially speaking as 'The Bug Hut'. This small picture house,

which functioned until the 1950s, was situated on the south side of Britannia Street (and known originally as The Britannia Picture Hall), occupying the former premises of the Britannia Brewery. T Newton of Worsbrough Common ('Childhood Memories', 22.10.93) remembered the Britannia opening when admission was 'a pound empty jar plus a penny for the rear. And woe betide the pianist if it was a bad film — she was more in danger than the Indians in cowboy films…[and] many elderly people paid someone to read the subtitles…it [often] sounded more like a pub tap room rather than a cinema'.

Even from the air the Alhambra Cinema, situated at the junction of Wesley Street and Doncaster Road had an imposing presence, outshining all other buildings in

Left: The St John's Church. *(Barnsley Archive Service)*

sight. In the week beginning 5 June 1939 the 'double-feature' programme consisted of Ray Milland and Olympe Bradna in the comedy *Say It In French* whilst *Arrest Bulldog Drummond*, an adventure involving international spies, starred John Howard and Heather Angel. Like its new rival, the Ritz, it had a

Above: The Alhambra Orchestra taken shortly after the opening in 1915. **Right:** Queuing at the Alhambra/Odeon Cinema, 1950s.

Saturday morning show for children. Laurance Richardson of Granville Street, remembered 'a little song to sing along with words like: "From far and near we've gathered for the picture show ('Childhood Memories', 24.9.93)".

The Alhambra was originally built in 1915 as a 2,600 seat theatre, the creation of Barnsley surveyor and architect Mr P A Hinchcliffe, who five years earlier had designed the Cudworth Palace of Varieties (destroyed by fire in 1927). The Alhambra's flamboyant frontage in white Faena stone, with a statuary figure supporting the Wesley Street corner of the building, may have been a parody of Classical or Renaissance style but was a magnificent example of late 'Edwardian' theatre architecture.

The opening night, Friday 1 October, was a glittering 'high society' occasion, when parties of the principal guests occupied balcony boxes. They included Countess Fitzwilliam of Wentworth Woodhouse (who performed the opening ceremony which was followed by a charity concert on behalf of the Soldiers' and Sailors' Help Society); Baroness Beaumont of Carlton Towers; Mr and Mrs Scott-Smith of Banks Hall (Cawthorne); Countess Wharncliffe of Wortley Hall; Mr and Mrs Fullerton of Noblethorpe Hall (Silkstone); Sir Richard and Lady Pilkington of Chevet Park; Miss Spencer-Stanhope of Cannon Hall; the Mayor and Mayoress (Hon. Col. and Mrs W E England); Major and Mrs Carrington; Captain McKenna; Lieutenant Hudson; Ryan and Foers; Mrs Hewitt (wife of Lt. Col. Hewitt); Miss Fountain of Birthwaite Hall; Miss Warde Aldham of Frickley Hall and Mrs Howard Taylor. The 'ordinary' inhabitants of Barnsley were said to have 'responded

Below: Ernest Barker in pageboy uniform, Alhambra Cinema, 1932. *(E. Barker)*

Below: Some of the Alhambra staff in 1932, young Ernest Barker in the foreground. *(E. Barker)*

Below: The Alhambra Projection Room. Ernest Barker (left) and D. Callaghan. *(E. Barker)*

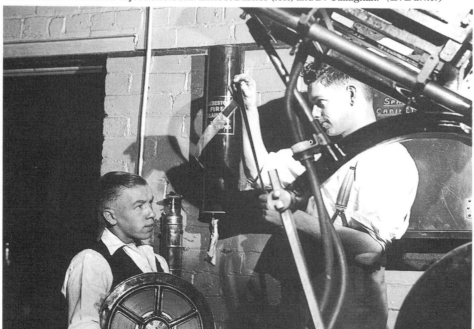

very well', some parts of the theatre 'being crowded'. The chief attraction was contralto Miss Phylis Lett, 'in fine voice', accompanied by the Alhambra Orchestra under the direction of Mr Cunningham. Hinchcliffe's dream of attracting stylish revues was ruined by a shortage of touring companies during the First World War, so music hall shows were introduced. Competition from the two other live theatres of the town — the Theatre Royal and Empire — hastened the Alhambra's conversion into a cinema in 1926.

The Alhambra became part of the Gaumont circuit of films and when the new Gaumont, in Eldon Street, opened in the 1950s was re-named 'The Odeon' but closed on 26 November 1960. Between 1962-c.79 the building was used as a bingo hall and subsequently remained empty until demolition in the late 1980s. The Alhambra [shopping] Centre now commemorates a once great place of entertainment from the Golden Age of the Cinema.

Below: The Alhambra in its 'Bingo Era'.

When the aerial view was taken the Globe Picture House, New Street, was offering two main feature films. From Monday to Wednesday there was the new Max Miller comedy *Everything Happens To Me* and, for the second half of the week, Dick Powell co-starred with Olivia De Havilland in *Hard To Get*, described as 'far from being a musical picture of the routine type, for Dick sings only one song and it is introduced plausibly into the action of the the piece'. Described after its opening in 1914 as 'the new, cosy and thoroughly up to date picture house' and 'The Cinema Delux of the District', The Globe was one of the pioneering purpose-built Barnsley cinemas showing silent films. Like the Alhambra it was converted into a bingo hall in the 1960s until taken over, in a very poor state of repair, by the Barnsley Theatre Trust in 1981. Following

Above: The Globe Picture House. *(Tasker Collection)*

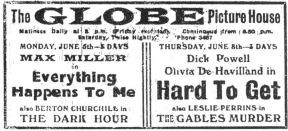

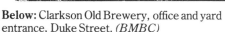

Below: Clarkson Old Brewery, office and yard entrance, Duke Street. *(BMBC)*

dedicated refurbishment it opened as the Globe Theatre in 1983 and for seven years hosted 110 amateur and professional productions, Barnsley Playgoers' *The Boyfriend* being its farewell performance. The frontage of this much-loved small theatre was 'in the way' of the

Western Relief Road and the cost of re-building was thought — by both Barnsley Council and the Barnsley Theatre Trust — to be too prohibitive, so in 1990 the whole edifice was demolished.

The lower part of Plate Ten provides us with a good view of Park Road, formerly part of the Doncaster-Saltersbrook turnpike. At its junction with Duke Street (extreme left) a large rectangular building is in view. This was part of the premises of Clarkson's Old Brewery, managed by William Coles Spooner. The former Park Road Junior and Infant School, at the junction of Beech Street can also be seen, its premises later occupied by the Barnsley College of Art.

One important building deserving our attention is the three-storey Model Lodging House which can be seen between Doncaster Road and Pontefract Road. First registered in the 1870s, it provided cheap and basic accommodation for the long-term homeless. The refuge had a 'timeless' atmosphere when in 1970 it was visited by Don Booker for his *Barnsley Chronicle* 'Other Side of the Fence' series. Sixty men and five women were in residence.

Below: The Model Lodging House, Doncaster Road.

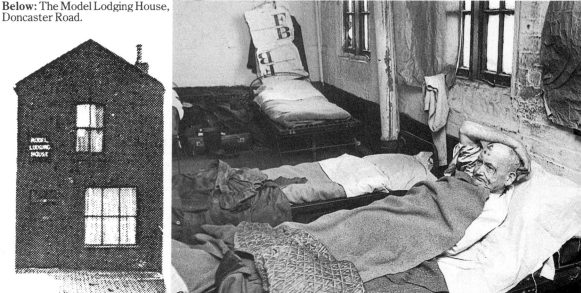

The relatively high aerial view (Plate 11) was taken on the same flight and similar direction as the previous example, providing us with a more distant image of the town at time when planned suburban development was taking place towards Highstone and Worsbrough Common. We are also given our first aerial glimpse of one of Barnsley's best known landmarks — Locke Park, located on the western part of an escarpment (running across the middle of the photograph) which reaches its highest point (575 feet) in the Recreation Ground at the top of Highstone Lane.

During the late 1930s the intriguingly named 'California Gardens', an area of allotments, South of Park Road, between Warren Quarry Lane and Tower Street was transformed into a new housing area, probably in two phases, including the creation of an access road — Highstone Avenue. Its American conotation may have been applied during or after 1848 when the 'Golden State' was 'in the news'. Mexico's cession of California to the U.S.A. was followed by the discovery of gold there, leading to a rapid influx of settlers.

The lower portion of the development (unnamed on the 1:10 000 OS map of 1938): California Terrace, California Street, California Crescent, Canada Street and Columbia Street appear, from the air, to be of more recent construction compared with properties at or near the top of the hill: Highstone Crescent and Avenue, Warren Crescent. Both portions contrast with the old suburban tradition of terraced courts and back-to-backs (featured in Plate 10) which can be seen to the North of Park Road; and also with the Edwardian terraces of West View, Tower Street and Highstone Road. The new houses were at a much reduced density,

Right: 1:10,000 O.S. map extract, 1938.

Below: Entrance and Lodge, Locke Park. The cannon was removed in 1928 and replaced with an ornamental vase. *(Elliott Collection)*

three-bedroomed, with kitchen, bathroom and garden. A more creative layout involved the use of crescents and closes and of course the introduction of the 'semi'. The development was part of the Corporation's scheme to accommodate families from sub-standard houses

Below: Locke Park Tower c. 1910. *(Elliott Collection)*

Below: Locke Park conservatory, Kingstone Church in the background. *(Barnsley Archive Service)*

around the centre of town. Allotment gardens sloping down towards Worsbrough, with their distinctive patchwork appearance so apparent from the air, were probably replacements for the loss of California Gardens. In the hungry thirties and subsequently during wartime and rationing these intensive plots provided welcome nourishment for many local families and were especially appreciated by miners.

Although out of view, the parish churches of St Edward the Confessor, Kingstone (1902) and St Luke's, Worsbrough Common (1874-5) served this area. St Edward's was formed from portions of the parishes of St John and St George.

Locke Park, with its tower and new bowling green easily recognisable, was understandably busy on a sunny Friday in early June. Less distinct is the bandstand,

just in view to the extreme left of the frame, the Lodge at the main entrance on Park Road, and the Fountain and Locke Monument at the beginning of the elongated wooded 'Quarry' area to the left of the bowling green.

The park occupied land formerly known as High Style Field. As late as circa 1860 the 'upland' edge of Barnsley, extending towards Worsbrough Common, was still perceived by many people as being a rather wild and inhospitable area — despite the enclosure of Barnsley and Worsbrough commons ten to eighty years earlier. This was understandable since much of its western extent, historically known as 'Barnsley Moor', was exploited for coal and stone from the fifteenth century and included the old Race Common. Barnsley's last horse-race meeting took place in High Style Field during Feast Week, 1859. The names Racecommon Lane and

Below: The Band Stand c. 1910. *(Elliott Collection)*

Below: Locke Park cafe and commemorative drinking 'fountain' *(Elliott Collection)*

Racecommon Road are reminders of a sporting tradition extending back to at least 1709.

There was a campaign during the late 1850s by the 'working men' of Barnsley to establish a 'People's Park', though the suggestion of High Style Field, with its 'uneven surface, and high, bleak, exposed situation' was not ideal, according to one correspondent of the *Barnsley Chronicle*. The anonymous writer thought that Shaw Lands 'a better site by far', and Church Field, 'an admirable site for a public promenade', even better.

The sudden death in 1860 of the great railway engineer Joseph Locke, aged 55, lead his wife, Phoebe, to present High Style Field to the Corporation of Barnsley in the form of a new public park in accordance with her husband's wishes. The land was enclosed, suitably landscaped and a house built for the keeper. The gift included a fund 'sufficient to insure its being preserved for the purpose for which it was intended'.

Although born at Attercliffe, Locke spent his formative years in Barnsley where his father worked as a viewer or mining engineer at Gawber Colliery, his attendance at the grammar school (now Cooper Gallery) from the age of seven to thirteen being his only formal education. In 1988 a plaque was reinstated on the site of Locke's childhood home in Shambles Street, above what was then the Lewis Wadsworth estate agency. The unveiling party included Deputy Mayor, Councillor Roy Warden, Sir Nicholas Hewitt, Chairman and Managing Director of the Barnsley Chronicle and former Barnsley resident Mrs Vicky Haworth of the Robert Stephenson Trust.

In 1819 young Locke left Barnsley and became apprentice viewer at Pelaw Colliery, County Durham where he became friendly with another teenage apprentice — Robert Stephenson. After two years Locke had become unhappy with his situation so returned to Barnsley where he found employment as under viewer and clerk at his father's pit but left Barnsley as an inhabitant for the last time in 1823. Within twenty-years he was regarded by his fellow engineers as the leading pioneer of the railway system. There is no doubt that Locke's contribution to the Railway Age has never been fully acknowledged compared with 'household names' such as Stephenson and Brunel. Yet he engineered more miles of railway line than anyone in Britain and founded the Continental rail system. Locke undoubtedly had a great affection for his home town and must have been cheered by the

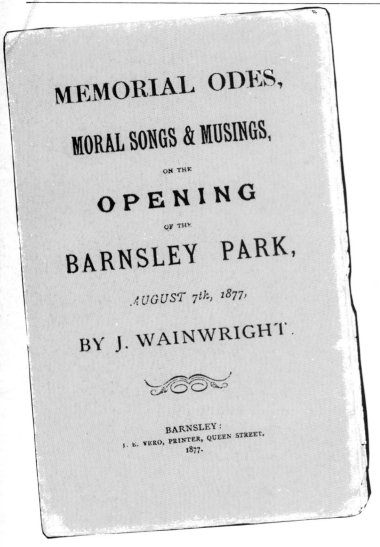

MEMORIAL ODES,

MORAL SONGS & MUSINGS,

ON THE

OPENING

OF THE

BARNSLEY PARK,

AUGUST 7th, 1877,

BY J. WAINWRIGHT.

BARNSLEY:
J. K. VERO, PRINTER, QUEEN STREET,
1877.

Burland was inspired to compose *Apotheosis of Joseph Locke* in honour of the man and the occasion:

ENWREATH our Townsman's head
  With the immortal bay,
  For amongst us he was bred,
    We all are proud to say.
Yoke the fiery prancing steeds
To the grand triumphal car,
Emblazoned with the useful deeds
Of talent — not of ruthless war;
Draw him along each crowded street
Of his banner-waving, bough-decked town;
Let hearty acclamation meet
His wide-spread, well-deserved renown.
    The illustrious Joseph Locke,
    Our Townsman great and good,
    Who cleft the primal rock,
    Who bridged the sweeping flood,
    Who bored the Alpine chain,
    Who filled up chasms deep,
    Who made the level plain
    Mid precipices steep,
Piercing mighty masses through,
For the girded iron way,
Which Roman could not do,
In triumph comes to-day.

Oppidans magnanimous! Emulate
His glorious deeds! Lagging in debate
Robs Action of the chances of success,
And makes the soul diminutive still less;
Thus mannikins and pigmies swarm around,
Where men of sterling merit should be found.
Seeing greatness is awarded fame, make
Yourselves renowned! In all you undertake
Strain every nerve and sinew to the task—
Not in the pleasant sunshine idly bask.
Follow Locke's example; and spite of Fate,
Make up your minds to be something — great!
    Along the Hero comes,
    In chariot fashioned old,
    With the dignity of Jove,
      And the mein of Roman bold.
      The vast procession moves
    To notes of music shrill,
    An ovation to the man
      Of intellect and will,
    Our Townsman Joseph Locke,
    Shedding lustre on us all
    By his majesty of port,
      And greatness of his soul:
      Open wide the gates!
    Let the hero enter in,
    Mid the Cannon's stunning roar
      And crowd's applauding din.
High Stile Field no more! This is now Locke Park,
Where Barnsley denizens may hear the lark,
The luxury enjoy of shrub and tree,
And perfume breathing flower! Ever free
Alike to rich and poor! A noble gift,
Won for us by hard mental toil and thrift!
A boon with pleasure, health, and beauty fraught!
So let us esteem it as we ought!

Above: 'The Pillars', Locke Park, once graced the portico of Commerce Buildings (now Royal Bank of Scotland) Church Street/Royal Street. *(Elliott Collection)*

'celebrity status' he received on return visits in the 1850s, becoming one of its most noted benefactors.

The park was opened amid great pomp and ceremony on June 10 1862, a 'Locke' commemorative medallion was issued and local historian and poet John Hugh

The Institute of Civil Engineers commissioned, from subscriptions, the Italian sculptor Baron Marochetti to create a bronze figure of Locke, their former president, and requested permission to place it beside those of Stephenson and Brunel in St Margaret's Garden, Westminster. It would have been a deserved honour for the man who was described in the *Times* obituary